THE REMAKING OF
KING'S LYNN

Also by the author:

The Beachmen

The Antiquities of King's Lynn

The Ingenious Mr Henry Bell

THE REMAKING OF
KING'S LYNN

Brown Brick and Rounded Corners

by
David Higgins

PHOENIX PUBLICATIONS

Published in 2008 by Phoenix Publications
Walnut Farm, Beech Crescent, West Winch,
King's Lynn, Norfolk, PE33 0PZ.
Tel: 01553 840447

Origination and printing by
Clanpress, King's Lynn, Norfolk, PE30 2ND.

© David Higgins, 2008.

The moral right of the author has been asserted.

All rights reserved. No part of this book may be reprinted or reproduced or utilised in any form or by any electronic, mechanical or other means, now known or hereafter invented, including photocopying and recording, or in any information storage or retrieval system, without the permission in writing from the publishers.

British Library Cataloguing in Publication Data
A catalogue record for this book is available from the British Library

ISBN 978-0-9540684-2-4

Contents

Preface	1
Town Improvement	
• The Making of a Town	3
• Early Attempts at Town Improvement	4
• The National Context	5
• A Paving Act for Lynn	6
The 1803 Paving Act (The First Act)	7
The 1806 Paving Act (The Second Act)	8
The Later Years	9
The Anatomy of Improvement	12
The Improvements	16
Town Expansion	
• Overview	47
• Phase I 1800-1820	47
• Phase II 1821-1845	49
• Phase III 1846-1855	53
The Anatomy of Expansion	58
The Expansion Areas	62
Epilogue	112
Appendix: Street Renaming, 1809	115
Sources	117
Notes and References	117
Bibliography	122
Index	123

ACKNOWLEDGEMENTS

I would like to express my gratitude to the following people and organisations for their generous assistance and support:

The staff of the King's Lynn Museums, the Norfolk Records Office (especially Susan Maddock), the King's Lynn Library and the Norwich Castle Museum.

Colin Barton and Elizabeth James, who both kindly made available the fruits of their own research.

Bob Booth, Rosemary Bryan, Reg Knights, Stan Langley, Paul Nichols, Bernie Ransom, Mary Smith, Phillida Smith, Peter Sykes, Jean Tuck, Jim Tuck and Desmond Waite for assistance with particular aspects of the research.

Robert Fuller of Robert Fuller Associates for scanning the illustrations.

Jane Whiskens of Clanpress for her patience and attention to detail.

Sheila West for typing the manuscript and assisting in other ways.

Brenda, my wife, for proof reading.

The illustrations in this book are subject to copyright and where not the property of the author are reproduced with the permission of the owners as follows:-

The King's Lynn Museums 3, 4, 6, 7, 11, 13, 18, 27, 30, 34, 35, 36, 38, 39, 40, 41, 42, 44, 45, 49, 55, 56, 57, 59, 61, 63, 64, 67, 69, 70, 71, 72, 73, 74, 75, 76, 77, 78, 80, 82, 87, 92, 100, 109, 110, 122, 123, 124, 125, 128, 130, 139, 148, 151, 152, 153, 154, 170, 174, 176, 177, 185, 186, 187, 188, 189, 190, 193, Front Cover, Back Cover
King's Lynn Borough Archives 8, 10, 23, 25
The Norfolk Record Office 12, 46, 48, 88
Jim Tuck 83, 121, 127, 171
Desmond Waite 37, 191
Bob Booth 94, 105, 114, 116, 172

Every effort has been made to trace other copyright holders and apologies are extended to any whose rights have been unwittingly infringed.

PREFACE

The London Overspill Agreement of 1962 sparked off a decade of rapid change in King's Lynn. The town was expanded by the creation of new housing and industrial areas and the town centre was redeveloped to provide new shops, car parks, service roads and other improvements thought necessary for the newcomers. At the same time steps were taken to clear areas of housing considered to be sub-standard.

At the outset it was well understood in academic circles that this would mean extensive demolition in the town centre and, as a result, the King's Lynn Archaeological Survey was set up to examine the origins and development of the mediaeval town through the study of historic buildings, archaeological excavation and documentary research.[1]

But as farsighted as this measure undoubtedly was, it was not enough for those who had to witness the destruction of large swathes of the town's historic fabric only to see it replaced by the monolithic Vancouver Centre and the Hillington Square development, the designers of which completely ignored the established character of the old town.

The insensitive manner in which this regeneration was carried out still rankles with many who were around at the time and the recent revamping of the Vancouver Centre has done little to help in this respect.

Contrast this with the fortunes of Lynn's first period of improvement and expansion carried out under the auspices of a group of men called the Paving Commissioners. Between 1803 and 1872, using powers conferred on them by local Paving Acts, these men reshaped the town in the name of improvement and oversaw a level of house building that doubled the town's housing stock.

By 1870 the mediaeval town, which had largely survived until 1800, had been transformed and expanded into one characterised by Georgian architecture or buildings designed in the Georgian tradition, fronted in a distinctive brown brick and featuring rounded corners.

This modernisation was welcomed at the time because in design terms it merely accelerated the gradual change in architectural fashion that had been taking place in the town for more than a century. To most it signified much needed progress.

Today the town as remade by the Paving Commissioners has become the 'old town'. Its good quality townscape and wealth of historic buildings are much admired and cherished by locals and visitors alike.[2]

This book tells the story of this little known yet important period in Lynn's development history. It is divided into two parts, town improvement and town expansion. Each contains an explanatory text and an illustrated 'tour' of the work carried out. I hope that by dealing with the subject in this way the reader will be able to take a fresh look at Lynn's old town and gain greater enjoyment through an understanding of one of the major forces that shaped it.

David Higgins
March 2008

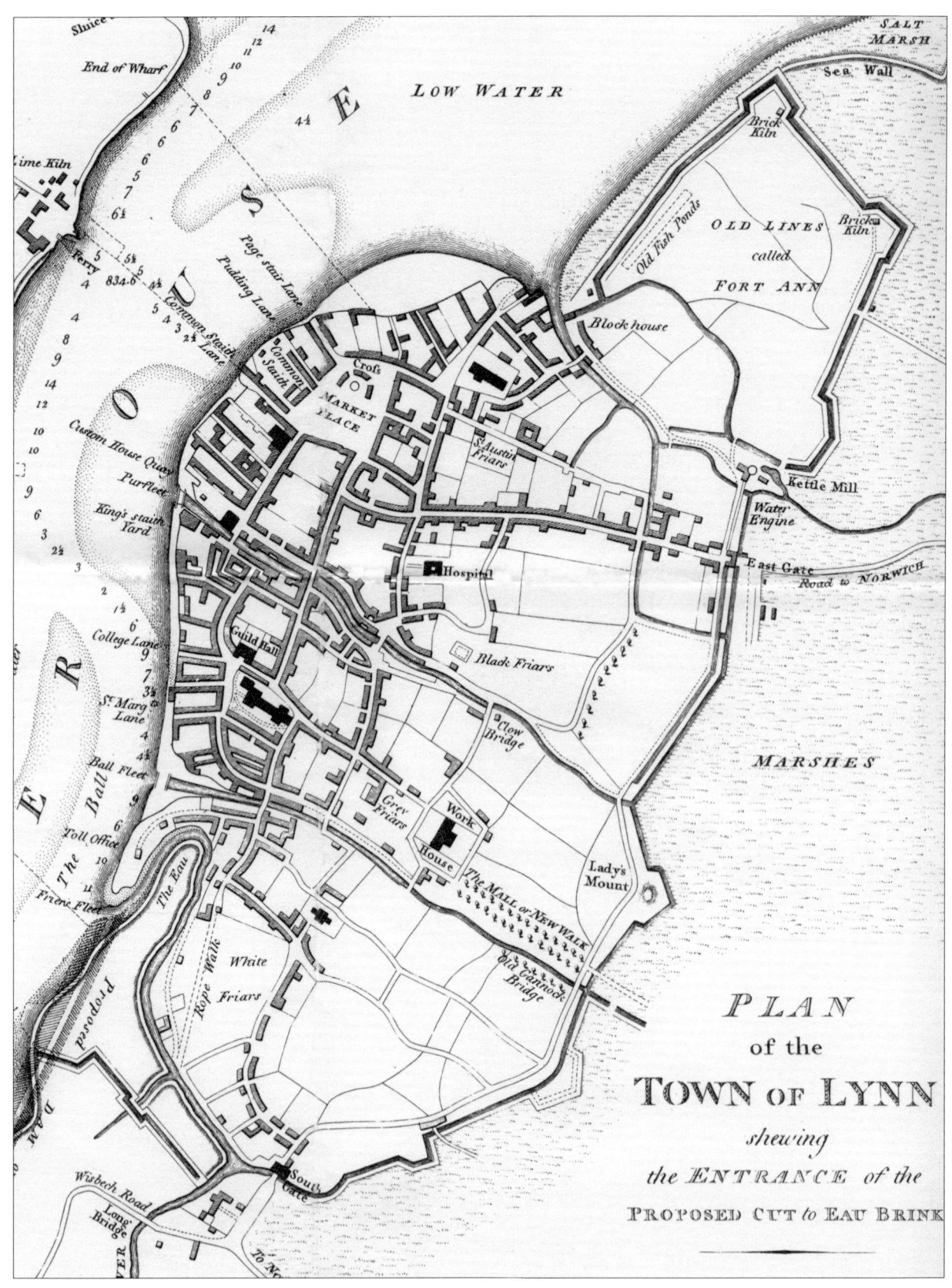

1. King's Lynn in 1797. The 'incommodious streets' improved by the Paving Commissioners. Inset from William Faden's Map of Norfolk.

TOWN IMPROVEMENT

THE MAKING OF A TOWN

The origin and development of King's Lynn is now well documented. Being at a point where sea, river and road transport met, the town was perfectly situated for trade, the driving force behind its subsequent prosperity.

The owner of the site was the Bishop of Norwich through his Lordship of the Manor of Gaywood; hence until the reforms of Henry VIII the town was known as Lynn Episcopi or Bishop's Lynn. By 1100 sufficient people had settled there to persuade the then Bishop, Herbert de Losinga, to build a church (St. Margaret's) 'at the request of all his sons around Lynn',[3] but before this was completed, he granted it, together with the profits of a market and a fair, to the monks of Norwich Cathedral Priory.

The town so granted was confined to an area between the Millfleet and the Purfleet, but success was soon to prompt expansion. This seems first to have taken place eastwards, towards the sea bank (the Guanock), which had protected an earlier reclamation from the estuarine lake or 'Lenn' for, by the end of the 1130s, St. James' Chapel had been built for the people living in that area.

Shortly afterwards land across the Purfleet, as far north as what was to become the first Fisher Fleet, was settled and around 1150 Bishop Turbe granted to the Cathedral monks a chapel (St. Nicholas) in his 'newland'. This time, however, the Bishop retained the duplicate secular rights of what was in effect a second new town, cheek by jowl with the first.

So successful were these towns that around 1200, by granting the monks similar privileges elsewhere, the Bishop regained possession of the first town and in 1204 King John granted the unified settlement a self-governing charter, creating in effect a town council, the nature of which was to remain more-or-less the same for the next 600 years.

Finally, in 1558, South Lynn, which pre-dated its larger neighbour, was incorporated into the Borough by a charter granted by Queen Mary, although it retained its separate ecclesiastical identity and still does today.

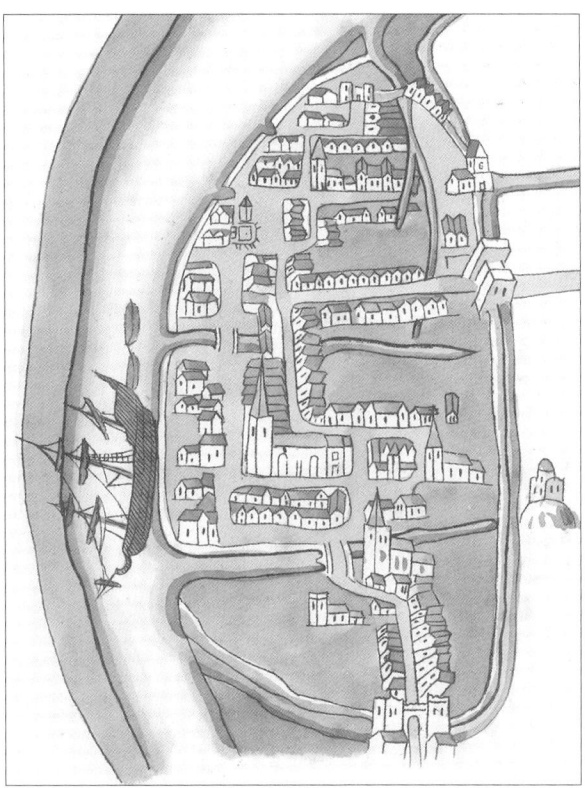

2. King's Lynn in the 1580s. Detail from a map of Castle Rising Chase.

But if the situation of the town was near perfect the site left a lot to be desired. Being a port it was of necessity set against the eastern shoreline of the Lenn, on salt-marsh raised above sea-level by accumulated salter's waste. This was not ideal building ground and much time and effort was expended protecting the fledgling town from marine and freshwater inundation and to keep it dry.

The most significant natural features on the site were the east to west flowing rivers and fleets. These were supplemented by many smaller man-made watercourses. This network of channels was variously used for transport, as a sewer system, as a source of power for mills and for 'fresh' water. More importantly for this study it greatly influenced the town's layout.

Between these watercourses lay a grid of streets, which, although irregular, has the appearance of a deliberate act of town planning, especially in the second new town. The east-west streets ran parallel to the fleets but those running north-south had to bridge them. At one time the Corporation had to keep as many as 25 bridges in repair.

This layout was well established by 1300. The only significant change to take place, before the early 19th century, was the virtual disappearance of the streets and houses around St. James' Chapel and the development of merchant premises on made ground to the west of the original quayline. It is shown clearly on the earliest map of the town, drawn in the 1580s and was virtually unchanged when 200 years later William Faden published his map.

3. The Seal of the Corporation of Lynn.

EARLY ATTEMPTS AT TOWN IMPROVEMENT

With the exception of some prestigious stone built properties along the waterfront, early Lynn was essentially a town of mediaeval timber-framed buildings. With no design discipline and with their characteristic jettied upper floors projecting over the street, the townscape these buildings presented was quite irregular, a perception heightened by the inevitable tendency for property owners to try to increase the size of their holdings by street encroachment.

The streets themselves were also a problem. Most were only partly paved and where paving did exist, it was provided by the individual frontagers with little regard for the street level as a whole.

To our modern eye this would have appeared picturesque, as Lavenham does today, but for the mediaeval merchant, for whom good communication was important, this was not an ideal situation. By the 16th century, however, the Corporation (comprised largely of merchants) had started to take steps to keep the streets and watercourses free from obstruction and to make the street elevations more uniform, given there was little scope for major redevelopment.

As far as individual buildings were concerned the Corporation had little power to compel owners to carry out improvements to the street elevations. The only useful statute that could be used was that for the Decay of Towns (1541), which enabled the Corporation to compel the owners of derelict property to carry out repairs. This statute was invoked in the 16th Century, but only three times.

For the streets themselves, by the late 16th Century there were attempts to limit encroachment and to fix and maintain a building line for each street. From 1560 the position of the front wall of any new property had to be agreed with the Town Chamberlain and those not conforming were ordered to be pulled down. In addition the process of 'latching', whereby walls were built under the first floor projection of a jettied building thereby producing a flush façade, was encouraged.

To deal with uneven street surfaces, in 1546 the Corporation ordered all the pavements throughout the town to be repaired and through the Court Leet it was possible to compel individuals to keep paving in repair. In 1571 it became an offence to lay new pavements above or below the general level of the street.

Through these public initiatives and the efforts of private individuals, the streets of Lynn gradually took on a more ordered and uniform appearance and the introduction of

4. Nelson Street, 1902. Jettied timber-framing alongside latching.

brick as a building material accelerated this process. In this way Lynn was brought closer to the Dutch style of townscape, which Lynn merchants knew from experience provided an encouraging environment for trade. In 1722 Defoe felt able to describe Lynn as a 'beautiful well built, and well situated town,…'. [4]

But the demand for improvement never went away and by the end of the 18th Century the prominent men in the town had decided it was time to deal with the problem in a more comprehensive fashion.

THE NATIONAL CONTEXT

The people of Lynn were not alone in deciding to take this course of action for, during the 18th Century, the country's urban elite had come to the collective conclusion that action was needed to improve the physical state of towns and cities.

The perceived problems were much more than the elements already referred to, i.e. encroachment, poor paving, and lack of uniformity in the street scene. Filth abounded in streets where livestock roamed free and there was no provision for public cleansing or refuse collection. In addition, at night towns were very badly lit, making it dangerous to venture out, there being no police force.

What was needed was a new type of public body, for the existing urban authorities lacked the power, resources or inclination to effectively manage town life. It will come as no surprise to learn that the first steps towards creating such a body started in the capital, where the problem was most acute. As early as 1662 a Public Act created a new local authority for the cities of London and Westminster. Commissioners appointed under this Act were empowered to make new sewers and remove nuisances and encroachments, but paving and lighting remained the responsibility of each householder. More critically the Commissioners were not given the power to levy a rate to carry out their functions.

Other Acts followed but not in any great number until the Liverpool Act of 1748. From then on there was a steady stream of local Acts establishing bodies of improvement commissioners (as they were generally known), a process accelerated by the Westminster Paving Act of 1762. Whilst retaining the obligation placed on householders to maintain existing pavements this Act empowered commissioners to pave new streets or repave old

5. George III in whose reign the Paving Commissioners did most of their improvement work.

ones to a systematic plan. It also authorised the funding of this work not only by tolls but also by a rate specifically levied for the purpose. It was the breakthrough that was needed.

Between 1748 and 1835, in practically every municipal borough of any importance, there was established a fairly uniform body of improvement commissioners with their own staff and funds. There were over 300 of these bodies charged with improving, paving, cleansing, lighting and watching. In most towns their importance far outweighed that of the existing urban authority and through their work in the 19th Century they are the true forebears of the modern day local authorities.[5]

A PAVING ACT FOR LYNN

On Monday 23rd August 1790 the principal inhabitants of Lynn assembled in the Town Hall to hear the Mayor, Henry Bell, give details of the cost of 'New Paving the Town of Lynn' and of 'the annual Expence of lighting, cleansing and watching the same'. He also outlined how the money might be raised to carry out this work.

The meeting was unanimous in its support for the ideas put forward and a committee was formed to prepare a Bill to place before Parliament for paving, lighting, cleansing and watching the town.

Flushed with enthusiasm the committee met two days later and under the chairmanship of the Mayor considered the estimates that had already been prepared by the Town Chamberlain, William Tuck. It was Tuck's view that the area of the streets to be paved together with the two market places measured some 63,000 square yards and that the cost of materials and labour for this work would amount to £8,086. To this he added a further £1,614 to cover lighting, drainage, the cost of obtaining the Act and other expenses. He also provided an estimate of the annual running costs.

On 8th September the committee resolved to finance the scheme by levying a rate not exceeding 2s 3d in the pound on all buildings and land in the Parish of St. Margaret's and to raise certain tolls.

In October the Corporation pledged £1,000 towards the cost of obtaining the Act and in December the draft Bill was produced. On 10th January 1791 a further public meeting resolved to place the Bill before Parliament. But not everyone was in favour of the proposed measures or, more precisely, the method of paying for them, the most significant among these being the country gentlemen, who had sufficient influence in Parliament to cause a Bill to fail, should they so wish.

Meetings were held between town and country representatives, to try to reach agreement but on 13th May 1791 the committee decided to postpone the submission of the Bill until the next session of Parliament. In the event nothing more is recorded about this first attempt to acquire a Paving Act and when the Town Clerk, Robert Whincop, presented an account for his work in connection with the Bill, he described it as 'by an Opposition thereto prevented from passing into a Law'.

The second attempt was launched on 1st May 1795, at a meeting convened by Mayor Edmund Rolfe Elsden at the request of the Grand Jury of the Quarter Sessions. The meeting resolved that 'the new paving of this Town is a Measure highly desirable, for the Accommodation both of the Town and Country; And that the Mayor be requested to invite the nobility, Gentry, Clergy, Farmers, and others interested, to meet the Inhabitants of this Town and unite with them in forming a Plan for carrying the above Measure into Effect'.

It was also resolved that the better cleansing, lighting and watching of the town would be desirable and that the inhabitants should solely bear the cost of these services.

Another meeting was held on 7th July, but this

6. The Town Hall where the Paving Commissioners conducted their business. From a drawing by John Farrington.

was adjourned without making progress and, like before, nothing further is recorded about this initiative. Despite taking great care to involve the country gentlemen from the outset it would seem that they had once more exercised their veto.

The third attempt, however, was to prove successful. On 25th March 1802, at a vestry meeting in St. Margaret's Church, it was decided to request the Mayor 'to consider of the Expediency of a General Pavement of the Town'. The Mayor duly convened a meeting of the townsmen on 2nd April 1802 at which it was agreed that the measure would be highly beneficial to both the town and country.

As a result, a Paving Committee was formed to prepare a plan to put before a meeting of the town and country. Mr. Farndon Groom of Boston was employed to prepare the plan. He estimated that paving the whole town would cost £8,879 8s 11d with an additional £1,000 for drains and grates. In addition the cost of the proposed new road from the South Gate to the end of St. James' Street was set at £676 for the road, excluding the value of the land, and for the associated bridge over the Millfleet, £554 14s.

On 6th January 1803 a meeting of the inhabitants of the town and of the neighbouring country considered the plan and the overall costs, which amounted to £13,500 capital with annual expenditure of £1,625. These estimates were approved and five country gentlemen were asked to withdraw with five gentlemen from the town to fix

7. Tower Street, c1910. Robert Whincop's house is on the left.

the proportion of the interest on the capital that should be borne by the country and the town respectively. This time agreement was reached, with the country paying a third and the town the remainder.

With the main obstacle to progress seemingly removed, the committee prepared a Bill and steered it through Parliament. The King's Lynn Paving Act received the Royal Assent on 17th May 1803.

THE 1803 PAVING ACT (The First Act)

The first Lynn Paving Commissioners were specifically nominated in the Act. They included the Mayor, Recorder, Aldermen and Members of Parliament, together with forty other named individuals. Not surprisingly the list included the Lynn notables of the day with the names of Bagge, Blencowe, Elsden, Everard, Hogge, Lane and Self to the fore, together with Robert Whincop, the Town Clerk, and the town's clergymen, Stephen Allen, Robert Hankinson and Edward Edwards. The Commissioners' eligibility depended on them being in possession of an estate valued at £100, or being an heir to someone having an estate valued at £200 or being in possession of a personal estate valued at £2,000.

To conduct the business, meetings were held each week in the Town Hall and a number of officers were appointed to carry out the work. These included a

8. Title block from the First Paving Act, 1803.

clerk, a treasurer, a surveyor, assessors, collectors and receivers of the rates. The first clerk was Robert Whincop Junior, nephew of the Town Clerk, and the first surveyor was the architect/builder Samuel Newnham, who resigned as a Commissioner to take up the post.

To finance their activities, the Commissioners were granted the power to levy a rate on the tenants or occupiers of property in the streets 'which shall be paved, cleansed, lighted, and watched,…'. The assessment mechanism was copied from that already in place for raising rates for the relief of the poor and the rate was not to exceed 2/- in the pound. Perhaps more significantly the power was also given to borrow money 'upon the Credit of the Rates'.

Turning now to what the Commissioners where required to do, it is instructive to look at the perceived need for improvement as set out in the preamble to the Act: 'Whereas the Streets, Lanes, public Passages, and Ways, within the Borough of *King's Lynn*, in the County of *Norfolk*, are not properly paved, cleansed, lighted, or watched, and are subject to various Nuisances, Annoyances, and Encroachments, and many of such Streets, Lanes, Passages, and Ways, are narrow and incommodious:' It goes on to state, 'And whereas it would tend greatly to the Benefit, Convenience, and Safety of the Inhabitants…, if these areas of concern were improved and measures put into place to prevent them recurring'.

This statement of the problem and the solution were common to most Improvement Acts but specifically mentioned in the Lynn Act was a requirement to create a new road from the South Gate into St. James' Street and the need to hold the Saturday Market and the Beast Market in more suitable locations.

It can readily be seen that the Commissioners were required to carry out functions that are now called town planning, building control, environmental health, highways, community services and police, hence the claim that the improvement commissioners were the pioneers of modern municipal work. Under the Act the Lynn Paving Commissioners set up an organisation to carry out street cleansing, street lighting, policing and the control of a whole variety of nuisances, but it is the work they carried out to change the physical appearance of the town that is our primary concern.

9. The Saturday Market today.

THE 1806 PAVING ACT (The Second Act)

Armed with the necessary powers the Paving Commissioners set to work, but their enthusiasm soon led to a significant Parliamentary post-script for within two years they had run out of money and were forced to seek the power to raise more.

The preamble to the Second Act describes the problem in the following terms; 'And whereas the Commissioners appointed by, or in pursuance of, the said [1803] Act, have made great Progress in the execution of the Powers thereby granted, and have expended the whole of the Money borrowed on the Security of the Rates authorized to be levied under the said Act, and have incurred a considerable Debt, which now remains due'.

On 4th September 1805 a meeting of the town's inhabitants decided not to support the raising of an additional rate, but by then the Paving Commissioners had already advertised the fact that they were going to petition Parliament for the powers to do so.

To back up their submission Samuel Newham, the surveyor, was instructed to prepare a note of the expenditure to date in implementing the First Act and an estimate of the cost of completing 'future Improvements which are desirable'. In addition his son, William, the town chamberlain, was commissioned to prepare a plan showing what work had been completed and what was yet to be done. [6]

The work completed, together with the cost, was specified as:- 'The New Road from Southgate £2,176 18s 5½d, Grey Friars adjoining the New Road £191 6s, Back Road from the late East Gate £289 18s 7d, Street Improvements £2,254 13s 10d, Lamps and Lamp Irons etc £420 8s 5½d, Scavengers (equipment) £209 6s 5d, New Paving £6,010 13s 1½d, and sundries £1,189 16s 1d' (including £848 4s 1d for the expense of obtaining the First Act). This amounted to £12,743 1s. To this was added a further £2,611 2s 10½d, the cost of carrying out lamp lighting, scavenging and watching to December 1805.

The future improvements included works to a number of properties in Purfleet Street, Baker Lane, Lath (Nelson) Street, Chequer (King) Street, Broad Street, Black Boy (Tower) Street and Dog (North) Street, together with the completion of the work in relation to the Trinity Chapel of St. Margaret's Church and to the Ladybridge, the estimated cost of the whole being £1,987 14s.

10. A handbill proposing opposition to the Second Paving Act, 1805.

We have already seen that opposition to acquiring the First Act was from the country gentlemen, there being little evidence that the townsmen were averse to the measure. This was not the case with the Second Act. Immediately after the town meeting a flyer was issued inviting the proprietors and occupiers of houses, lands and tenements in King's Lynn 'to adopt Measures for defeating so arbitrary a Stretch of Power by a liberal, open and manly resistance'.

On 9th September the opponents held a meeting at the Crown Inn in Church Street at which an action committee was formed under the chairmanship of the Rev William Winder. Several meetings followed and a petition of objection was drawn up to send to Parliament. It was even claimed that no other Paving Commissioners in the Country levied a rate of more than 2/- in the pound but, at the end of the day, their arguments were of no avail for the Act allowing the Commissioners to raise an additional 1/- in the pound gained the Royal Assent on 21st April 1806.

THE LATER YEARS

Work continued apace and by 1820 all the 'narrow and incommodious' streets, in fact the majority of the streets and bridges shown on Faden's map, had been surveyed, widened and largely new paved. When in 1836 William White described the impact of the Paving Acts he was able to say; 'By virtue of these acts, all the streets have been new paved, obstructions and other nuisances removed, and the avenue from the Southgate, instead of opening, as formerly, through the narrowest and worst built streets, has been diverted in a direct line more to the east, and now presents to the

11. Mr. J. J. Coulton (seated) beside the Clifton House Tower, c1905. Also pictured, Miss Coulton and Mr. R. C. Coulton.

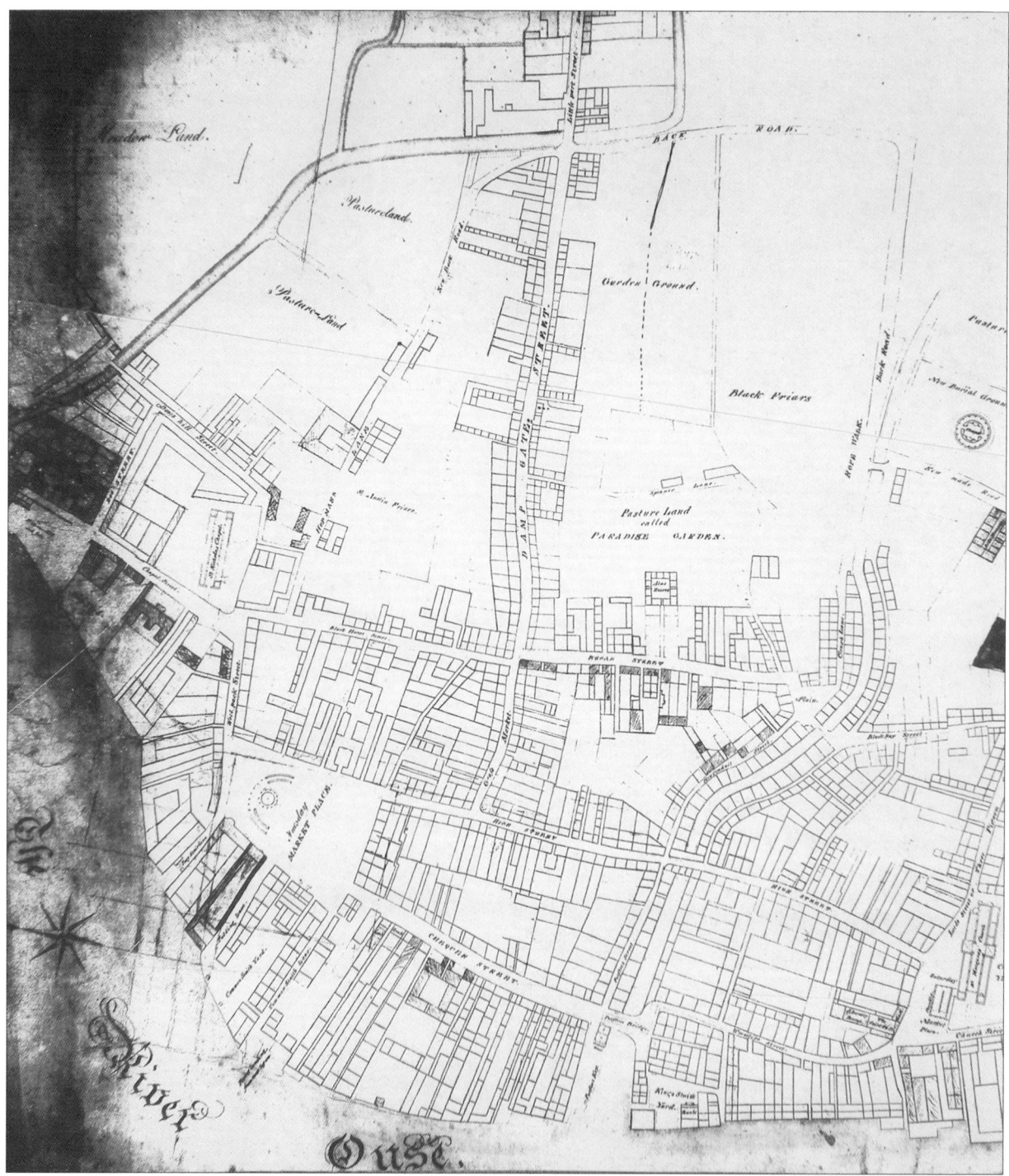

12. A Plan of the completed improvements and those yet to be carried out. William Newham, 1806.

traveller an approach superior to that of most other maritime towns in the kingdom; being a broad and spacious street (called London road), lined with handsome modern houses, terminated at one end by the venerable entrance gate, and at the other by the slender, but elegant and lofty hexagonal tower of the Grey Friary. The bridges over the "Fleets" have been made lower and wider, and the communication over Purfleet bridge, near the Custom - house, has been opened for carriages'.[7]

Until then the aims of the improvement commissioners nationally had been to improve the convenience of movement around cities and towns and to secure greater protection of life and property.

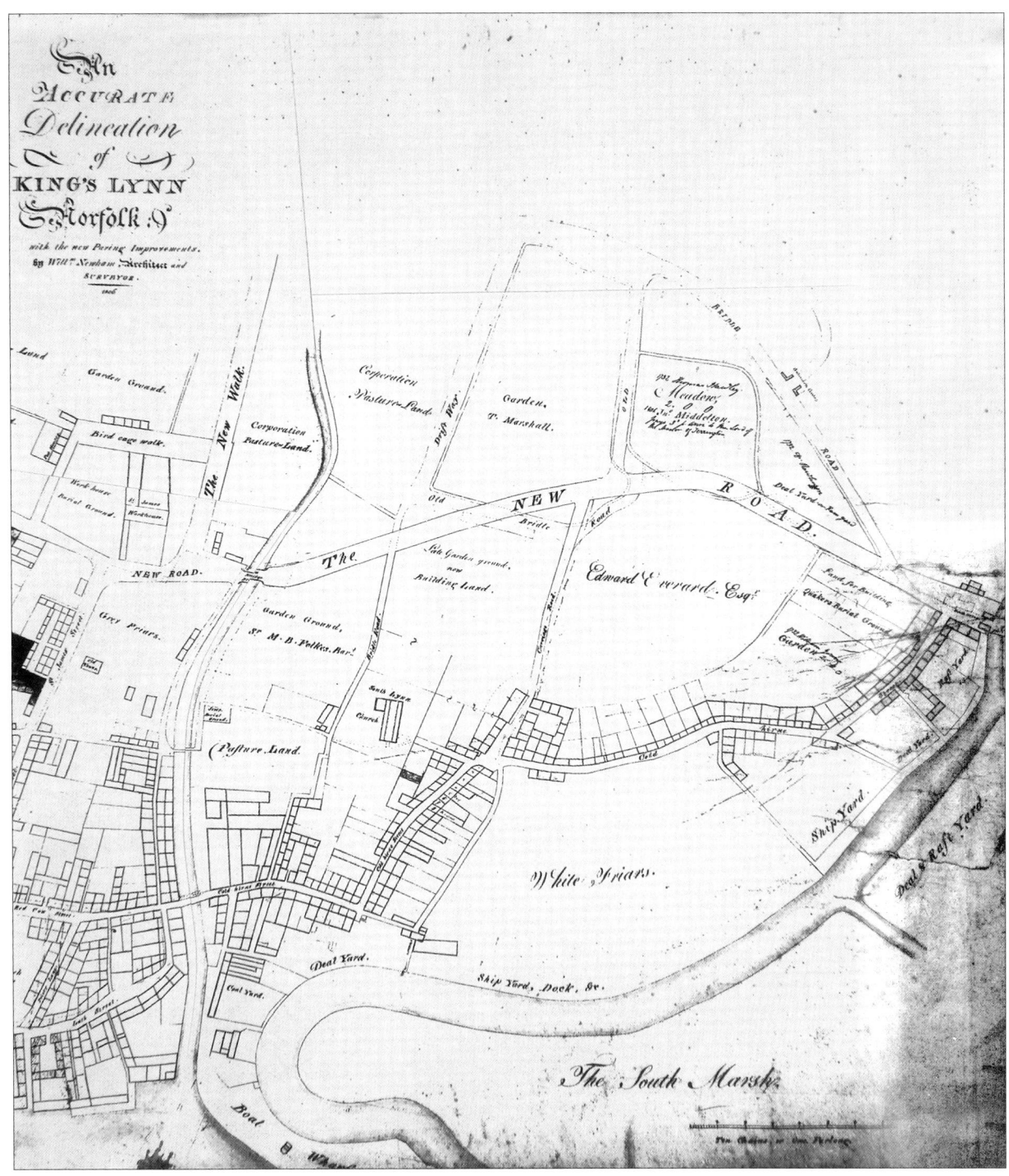

There was no suggestion that any of their work was carried out for reasons of public health.

All this changed after the cholera epidemic of 1831-3, which killed many thousands of people and those of 1848 and 1854 which killed many more. Town improvement then ceased to be merely desirable as a means of achieving ease of movement; it became a necessity on the grounds of public health.

The Municipal Corporations Act of 1835 provided the first challenge to the role of the Paving Commissioners, but its provision for them to merge with the new town councils was only permissive and, as far as Lynn was concerned, there was no willingness to do so.

Between 1848 and 1854 the process of merger was accelerated by pressure from the Board of Health. Each time it made an order to apply the Public Health Act to a town, it sought to amalgamate the commissioners and the town council.

Such was the case when in 1852 William Lee came to Lynn to hold an 'Inquiry into the Sewerage, Drainage, and Supply of Water, and the Sanitary Condition of the Inhabitants of the Borough of KING'S LYNN…'. Lee took extensive evidence including that from John James Coulton, in his twin capacities of Superintendent Registrar and Clerk to the Paving Commissioners. Predictably Lee recommended that the Act should be applied to the Borough and that the Commissioners and the Corporation should merge. [8]

As a result the Mayor called a public meeting at which it was unanimously agreed that the Act should not be applied. The debate on this matter continued until 1856 but shortly afterwards the work commenced on drafting a new Act which gained the Royal Assent on 19th April 1859 under the title: The King's Lynn, Waterworks, Markets and Borough Improvement Act. This incorporated many of the most important clauses of the Town Improvement Clauses Act of 1847, thereby constituting the Paving Commissioners a quasi Board of Health.

In this role, between 1864 and 1866, they carried out the filling in of the Purfleet and the related widening of New Conduit Street. It was to be their last major project, however, for under the Public Health Act of 1872 their powers were finally transferred to the Corporation.

THE ANATOMY OF IMPROVEMENT

During their period of office the Paving Commissioners made, or inspired, many individual changes to the town's fabric, which collectively transformed the look of the town. These changes will soon be considered in some detail but before doing so it will prove instructive to consider a number of key aspects, which shaped the improvement process as a whole. These concern the methodology by which the streets were improved, the paviors and the nature of the paving, the design of buildings and the materials used, the application of building regulations and the naming of streets and numbering of houses.

Street Improvement Methodology

It is clear from their early activities that the Commissioners main objective was to improve movement around the town by widening the principal streets and clearing them of superficial obstructions. To accomplish this their surveyor was tasked with producing a plan for each, showing a proposed improvement line. From the written evidence and the only plans to have survived it can be seen that these improvement lines were very precise. Some required the façade of a building to be demolished and set back to gain as little as one foot of ground for the street.

Once the line had been fixed the affected owners were offered a sum of money (representing the estimated cost of the work) and instructed to set their facades back. In default the Commissioners could carry out the work for them. The owners were, however, awarded compensation for the loss of their land, which usually was calculated at 10s per

13. Norfolk Street, 1891, showing a setted carriageway and flagged footways.

square foot.

In respect of the structures, which were considered to be encroachments, the owners were ordered to remove them at their own expense.

The final element of the process was the provision made for the continued widening of the streets as owners of buildings not originally affected chose to rebuild their properties. In these circumstances the Commissioners paid the standard rate for ground added to the street. This was a popular measure attracting a lot of interest in the decades following the initial work.

Paving and Paviors

Once the streets were widened and the encroachments removed the roadways were paved, creating a central carriageway of cobbles or setts with raised flagged footways on either side. For many this distinction was an innovation.

As previously mentioned Farndon Groom of Boston was employed to prepare the estimate for new paving the town and it was to him, on 20th June 1803, that the first contract was awarded. This involved taking up any old paving and laying new paving in what are now called St. James' Street, the Saturday Market Place (street only), the High Street and Norfolk Street.

Whether his work was unsatisfactory or he was subsequently unavailable is unclear, but whatever the reason, on 26th March 1804 the Commissioners sent for William Popjoy of Southwark to provide an estimate for paving the remainder of the Borough. It was Popjoy who completed the work, but it was not all plain sailing for in November 1806 he was paid £50 compensation 'in Consequence of the Paving Works being stopped for want of Money during the Course of the last Winter'.

As there were no local materials suitable for paving purposes, the bulk of what was needed had to be imported and throughout the period ships unloading paving materials at the Common Staithe Quay were a regular sight.

In the main the materials were shipped in from Scottish quarries, (granite for carriageways from Aberdeen and flags for footways from Castle Hill,

14. St. Margaret's Lane. A surface of granite setts probably laid in 1847 and still in use today.

Caithness), but occasionally materials were brought in from other places, such as cargoes of pebbles from Spurn Head.

Building Design and Materials

The style of architecture prevalent during the 70 years of the Paving Commissioners is generally termed Georgian or in the Georgian tradition. Variations in detail produced sub-styles such as Regency and Victorian but the basic characteristics remained the same throughout the period.

Each building façade presents a vertical profile to the street and is rectangular in shape or made up of a series of rectangles. This is in sharp contrast to the timber framing that, in the main, it replaced.

Roofs are pitched and covered in Welsh slate although for houses built before 1820 pantiles are the norm. Windows are of the double sliding sash variety, set back a few inches from the façade. Front doors often have doorcases and fanlights.

This gives a general impression of what the buildings of the period look like. More specific pointers are provided by the nature of the brickwork and the treatment of street corners.

One of the most obvious features of the old town

15. 1-2 St. Margaret's Place. Spot the brown brick interloper.

is the extensive use of brown brick for façades. This was clearly seen as a prestigious material for it is usually to be found in conjunction with the less costly 'Norfolk reds', which were used for flank and rear walls. Brown brick makes its appearance in Lynn around 1800 and was used until the early 1860s. By then it was less fashionable and could not compete with the cheapness of bricks brought in by rail. The brown bricks were made in local brickyards from Kimmeridge clay.

Less extensive and obvious are the façades built in gault brick. This brick was yellowish white when first laid but has since weathered to a dull grey.

There was no specific stipulation in either Act that buildings at street junctions should have rounded corners but it clearly was a requirement of the Commissioners and the large number that exist, both large and small, bear testimony to the fact.

Building Regulations

One of the age-old concerns of urban authorities was the everpresent risk of fire. The Great Fire of London of 1666 is well known, but many provincial towns suffered the same fate at one time or another.

From at least 1572 thatch as a roofing material was banned from the town and this prohibition was repeated in both Paving Acts. The First Act also included, as a fire protection measure, a clause, which in effect meant that all party walls in new buildings should be at least 9 inches thick and built of brick or stone.

This requirement was greatly expanded in the Second Act, as it had 'been found ineffectual for answering the purposes intended'. All external walls were then to be at least 9 inches thick and where a new building abutted an existing one, a separate gable had to be built of the same thickness. All these walls were to be of brick or stone. In addition, where terraces were being built, the party walls between every two houses had to be 9 inches thick, of brick or stone and built from the ground though the roof. These protruding firebreaks, usually capped by slate, are a useful feature to identify buildings built in the town after 1806.

17. Dated hopper head.

Prior to the Paving Acts it was common for rainwater running off roofs to disgorge into the street via gutter spouts. To remove this nuisance it was stipulated in the Second Act that for new buildings rainwater had to be taken to the ground in downpipes. Some downpipes already existed, as dated hopper heads attest, but the new regulation seems to have introduced, for the houses of the wealthy at least, a relatively standard lead pipe with a characteristic half funnel shaped hopper head. This functional yet attractive design had, in the country at large, been around for many years but the Lynn dated examples are all from after the Second Act. [9] Many of these are still to be seen in the town.

Finally, in order to enforce these regulations, it was stipulated in the Second Act that 24 hours notice had

16. Roof-top party-wall firebreaks.

to be given to the Commissioners' surveyor of any intention to build so that he could inspect to ensure compliance with the Acts.

Needless to say the builders were not always willing to follow the regulations and they were regularly reported to the Commissioners for non-compliance. Ironically these cases provide useful information on the construction dates for the buildings concerned.

Street Naming and House Numbering

The First Act conferred on the Commissioners the power to name streets and number houses. By the beginning of the 19th Century many of the existing street names were archaic and others seemed no longer appropriate, particularly those that took their names from prominent public houses. Several others had no commonly used name at all.

With the priority given to the town's physical improvements, it was not until February 1807 that the Commissioners turned their attention to this particular section of the Act, using it to comprehensively review and modernise all the town's street names.

A committee was formed for the purpose of 'new naming the Streets and Lanes in this Borough', but such were the sensitivities of the issue that it deliberated for two years before, on 10th March 1809, placing its recommendations before the Commissioners. The decisions made at that meeting and subsequent ones on 14th April produced the street names which exist today.

With Britain engaged in the Napoleonic Wars (1803-15) patriotism was to the fore. This is reflected in such names at King Street, Queen Street and, of course, Nelson Street. (The Duke of Wellington was not accorded recognition via a street name until after his death and then he was given five!). The county is acknowledged in Norfolk Street and the link to the capital in London Road. Other new names related to what were seen as more seemly local associations, with most of those named after public houses giving way to saint's names or ones related to an ecclesiastical feature.

Once approved the names were painted in black letters on a white background on conspicuous parts of the buildings at the ends of each street. (The full list of old and new names is given as an appendix).

Such dramatic change, however, was not to everyone's taste. The historian William Richards, complained that; 'The names of many of the Streets of the town were this year most capriciously,

18. King Street, c1905. Prior to 1809 this was called Chequer Street.

childishly, and confoundedly changed; and the rage of changing names appeared now so predominant, that some began to expect no less than that the town itself was to receive a new name'. [10]

Having renamed the streets, it would seem logical to have immediately set about numbering the houses, but this was not the case. It was not until October 1827, when the Board of Guardians asked for the houses in the parish of St. Margaret's to be numbered, to make it easier for them to collect the poor rate, that the Commissioners attended to the matter.

In August 1828 the names of the yards were also painted up so that the houses could be numbered, thus completing the task of making it easier to locate people in the town.

THE IMPROVEMENTS

It is now time to take a close look at the changes made. The most convenient way to do this is by way of a notional walking tour of the streets, as they existed in 1804, shortly after the completion of the New Road. The tour will focus on the work of the Paving Commissioners, but will also highlight changes made by other agencies, such as the Corporation and the Church, as well as noting other significant new buildings.

The route taken is shown on a map using Faden's 1797 work as the base and, where possible, the accompanying illustrations have been chosen to show the town after the Commissioners had completed their activities, but before subsequent demolition had blurred the image. The street name headings are those of today, but where they were different within the period 1803 to 1809 the old name has been given in brackets.

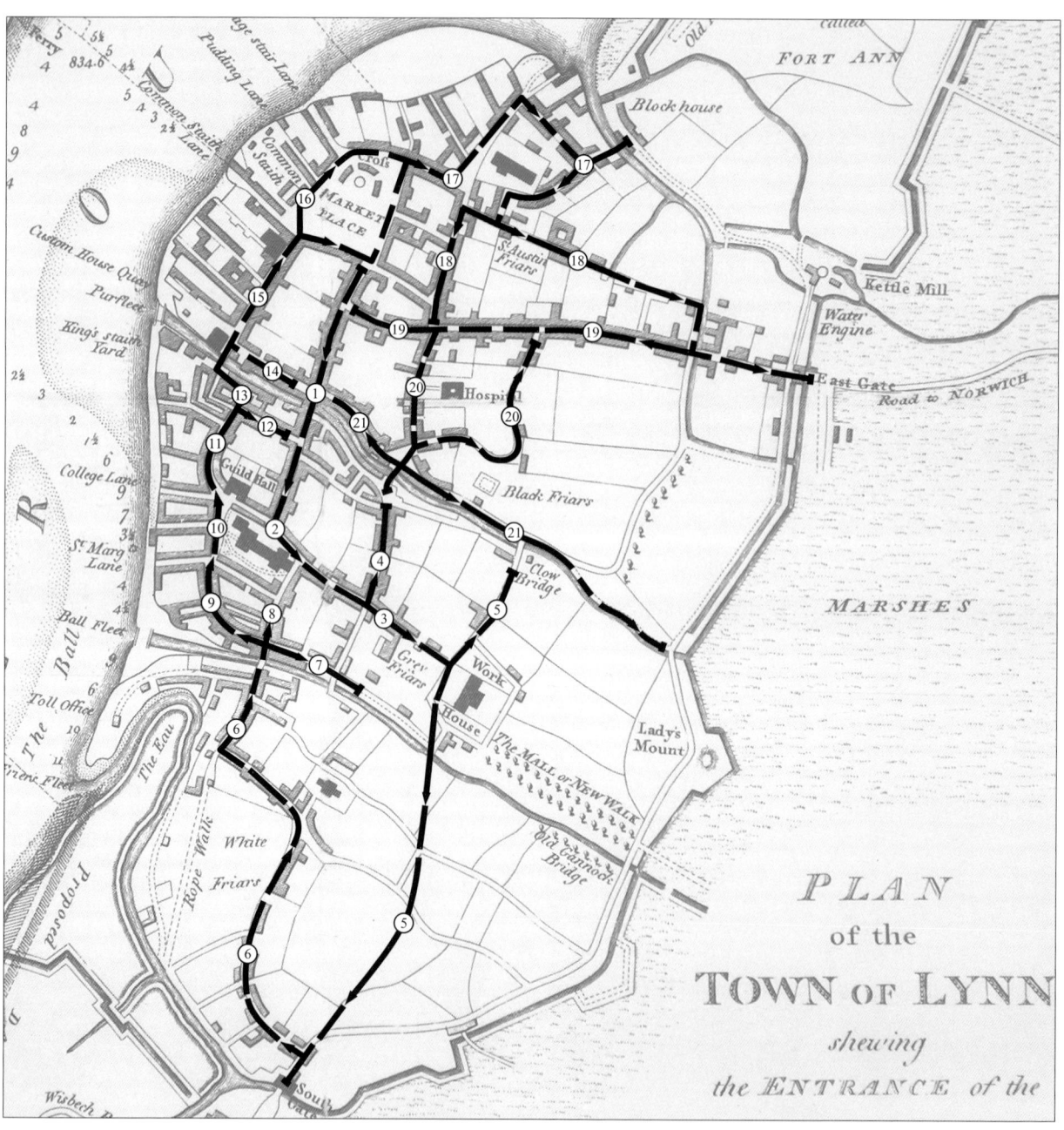

19. The Tour. Plan showing the route taken from the High Street (1) to New Conduit Street/Purfleet (21).

The High Street (1)

The evidence of prints and photographs, together with discoveries made within the refronted buildings, show that in 1803 the High Street was essentially mediaeval in character with many timber-framed buildings projecting over the street at first and second floor levels. Being the principal

20. 76-80 High Street showing brown brick rebuilding. No 78 was built by William Salmon Rolin in 1848.

shopping street, there were also a number of stall-like structures, called bulks, attached to the buildings, which encroached on the carriageway. The extent of the problem was such that the High Street was the first to receive the improvement treatment and it can usefully serve as a practical example of the methodology outlined above.

On 13th June 1803 a committee was formed 'to take a view of certain messuages on the East Side of High Street and extending from Grass Market to and including the Messuage now of Thomas Cooper and to determine upon the Alteration proper to be made on the Fronts of those Messuages or any of them' (this refers to the section from Norfolk Street to the Tuesday Market Place, on the east side).

21. Dated hopper head.

The committee reported on 29th June having, with the surveyor, surveyed both sides of the street. It recommended the setting back of façades and the removal of several encroachments at a cost of £151 10s 4d. With this agreed, the surveyor was ordered to make the owners aware of what was required.

On 7th July two committees were set up to survey the remainder of the street, one for the stretch between Norfolk Street and the High Bridge (close to where Burton's now stands) and the other from there to the Saturday Market Place. Both reported on 5th August, the estimates being £349 6s 7d and £166 17s respectively.

By 28th May 1804 most of the work had been carried out for, on that date, a committee was appointed to assess the compensation for land taken to add to the street. This committee reported on 24th September, naming 14 owners. In all compensation totalling £340 6s 4d was agreed although three

22. 48-52 High Street showing brown brick rebuilding.

23. 123 High Street. Wenn's Corner before improvement. Sketch from the Smith case papers, 1804.

owners had no sum set against their names, they being described as 'attended with particular Circumstances'.

It is clear from Newham's 1806 Plan that the main areas where fronts were set back to achieve widening were on the east side, comprising the stretch between Norfolk Street and the Tuesday Market Place; either side of the junction with New Conduit Street, including the High Bridge; and at the junction with the Saturday Market Place. On the west side the stretch close to Wenns Corner was given the same treatment. In addition at least 10 encroachments were removed.

Most owners accepted their fate, but two, William Smith and William Parlett, did not and their cases are instructive in that they illustrate the important distinction there was between having part of the main structure removed or merely a later addition by way of encroachment. These two cases seem to have had the effect of testing the newly created system for few others came to court.

Smith's case covers both aspects. He was described as a gentleman of South Lynn and owned the premises at the south-west corner of the High Street and Saturday Market Place (now No 123, Wenns). The Commissioners wanted Smith to do two things, to set back the front of that part of the building which faced the High Street by 1 foot 3 inches at the northern end and 2 feet 6 inches at the south, the whole being 45 feet 10 inches long, and to remove a building projecting upon the footway, fronting the Saturday Market Place and measuring 20 feet 9 inches by 4 feet 6 inches.

The former was in the occupation of Francis Hillyard. Ann Carter occupied the part to which the latter was attached. The Commissioners deemed both parts of the building encroachments and projections and, as such, compensation was not payable for the ground taken. With Smith disagreeing, the matter was referred to the Quarter Sessions for adjudication.

The verdict was given on 16th April 1804. The part occupied by Ann Carter was deemed an encroachment and consequently liable to be removed without compensation, whereas that occupied by Hillyard was adjudged not to be and the Commissioners were ordered to pay Smith

24. 123 High Street. Wenn's Corner as improved.

£27 10s compensation for the loss of the ground. They were also instructed to 'forthwith take down, take away and remove at their own expense…' the façade of the building, with the important stipulation

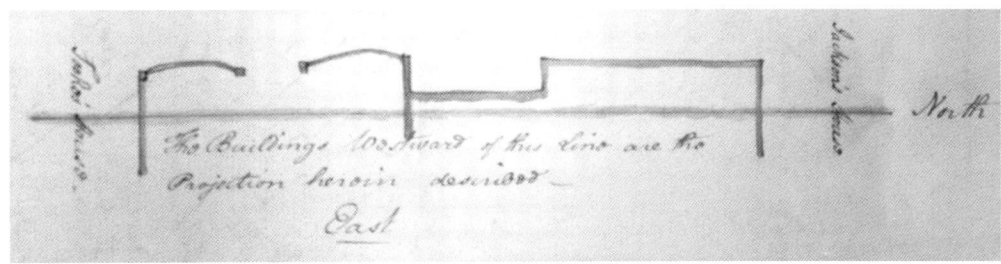

25. 38-39 High Street. Improvement line relating to William Parlett's premises, as depicted in the case papers of 1805.

given for the stretch north of Norfolk Street to be paved with granite 'so soon as the Mayor and Burgesses shall have replaced the Water Pipes'.

With the obvious obstructions removed it was now time for the gradual process of further widening as private owners redeveloped or refronted their premises. Much of the High Street owes its present character to this process as is evidenced by the number of brown brick façades, but the last timber-framed building was not demolished until the 1960s.

Two of these private initiatives are worthy of notice because of their prominence in today's street scene. The first is the building that stood at the south-east corner of the High Street. This fine three storeyed timber-framed house was reputed to have belonged to Walter Coney, a prominent late 15th Century merchant. In 1804 it was owned by John Coward, a brazier, who received compensation for relinquishing 28 square feet to the street. This is a small amount of land and probably represents an early rounding off of the corner without the demolition of the whole building.

Shortly before 1816 Samuel Newham, the Commissioners' surveyor, bought the property from

26. 36-39 High Street. Parlett's rebuilt premises are on the left.

that the rebuilding of the corner should be in a circular form.

William Parlett, a linen draper, owned premises on the site of what is now 38/39 High Street. These projected in front of the adjoining buildings. He was offered £50 12s 6d as the estimated cost of rebuilding his front wall in line with those of his neighbours, together with a 'reasonable' amount of compensation for the ground to be given up. He did not find the offer acceptable and so the Commissioners referred the matter to the Quarter Sessions. On 29th April 1805 the verdict was given. Parlett was awarded £43 3s 4d for the ground lost to the street (at the usual rate) together with £5 for his expenses. In turn the Commissioners were told to carry out the work at their own expense.

With the road widened, the next stage was to pave the street, but it seems that the High Street was already reasonably well paved for there is no record of new paving until 28th May 1821 when the order was

27. 1 High Street. The house reputed to have belonged to Walter Coney. Wash sketch by the Rev. Edward Edwards, c1800.

Coward's widow. Newham demolished the building and offered his employers, 58½ square feet of ground for street widening for £60, over twice the normal rate. The Commissioners thought his demand 'most exorbitant' and offered him 20 guineas. This he refused but some accommodation was eventually reached, involving the extinguishment of an ancient reserved rent. The resultant new building was constructed with a rounded corner.

The other example concerns the largest curve of them all, that at the north-eastern corner of High Street and Norfolk Street, a building now occupied by O^2. The case is something of a hybrid because although the Commissioners did not require a major improvement at the outset they later took the opportunity to achieve one.

In February 1854 James Tuck, owner of the building which stood at what was then called Eldred's corner (after the occupier, tobacconist Murray Eldred), approached the Commissioners with a view to them buying the freehold for street widening in consideration of an annuity for him and his wife, for life. The Commissioners did not take him up on the offer.

By April the property was in the ownership of John Sheppard he having, it would seem, settled an annuity on the Tucks.[11] Sheppard in turn offered to sell to the Commissioners all or part of the site. He produced a plan for rebuilding, which included 'throwing about One hundred and thirty square feet at the corner into the street...'. The Commissioners agreed the plan, subject to the corner being rounded but could not agree a price. In 1857 Sheppard unsuccessfully tried again.

In 1864 John Judd became the third owner to approach the Commissioners, with an offer to sell but, to his dismay, they decided instead to compulsory acquire the property because the annuities were still being paid to the Tucks. The value of the site was set at the Quarter Sessions at £100.

By January 1865 the building had been taken down, the corner widened and the remainder of the site enclosed. A purchaser was sought for the site but only one, Joseph Cox, showed any interest. His offer of £120 was accepted and in July 1866 he took possession. The building currently on the site was erected shortly thereafter.

The other interesting structure in the High Street to get 'the treatment' was the High Bridge (over the Purfleet). This is described in the Purfleet section.

28. 1 High Street. Building constructed in 1816 on the site of Coney's House.

29. 56 High Street. The largest rounded corner of them all.

The Saturday Market Place (2)

30. Saturday Market Place, 1901. The street was cleared of stalls in 1804.

Wenns and the building on the opposite corner are numbered as part of the High Street but their visual impact is more marked in the Saturday Market Place. Conversely, by 1803, the Saturday Market had a major impact on the High Street and the First Act made specific provision for confining it to the area now known as the Saturday Market Place. At this time the weekly market filled this area, the adjacent street from the Town Hall to the White Hart Inn, and the High Street as far as Union Lane, a stretch then called High Street Saturday Market, 'to the great Inconvenience of the Inhabitants and of the Public in general…'. [12]

Given their aim to improve circulation in the town the Commissioners saw clearing these streets of stalls as something of a priority, but there was a problem, for the frontagers gained a steady income from allowing stalls to set up and trade in front of their premises. This was called 'stallage' and extinguishing this right would require compensation.

The solution was set out in the Act. It was presumed that once the market was confined, the Corporation would be able to charge higher tolls, as there would be fewer pitches, and that this increase over 15 years would pay for the compensation.

Accordingly on 28th May 1804 the Commissioners' clerk was ordered to give notice to those affected to produce a written account of how much stallage they had received in the past seven years and to seek from the Corporation the probable annual increase in tolls.

It took until 28th February 1805 to decide that the Corporation should pay £900 to the various claimants by way of compensation, but by then the market had already been restricted to its present area.

A survey of the northern frontage of the Saturday Market Place was (with other streets) ordered on 29th June 1803. In the event little improvement was deemed necessary, but subsequently several of the buildings were refronted, especially in the 1840s.

The creation of the New Road (London Road) and the widening of part of St. James' Street to create a more convenient route into the centre will be described shortly. This route entered the Saturday Market Place at a point where the Sexton's House and the late 15th Century Trinity Chapel of St. Margaret's Church, combined to create a pinchpoint. [13]

On 7th July 1803, a committee was formed to 'effect the proposed Plan for widening and improving the Passage between the North East Corner of Saint Margaret's Church and

31. 9 Saturday Market Place. Brown brick with a touch of the neo-classical.

the Opposite Houses…'; and, as ecclesiastical property was involved, it wisely comprised the Reverends Allen, Edwards, Hankinson and Burn.

Tasked with 'obtaining the Concurrence of all interested parties', these clerics quickly placed the matter before the church authorities. On 25th July 1803 a meeting of parishioners resolved; 'That the House called The Sexton's House standing on the North Side of the Chancel of this Church be forthwith taken down for the Purpose of widening the Public Street there'. This small building stood on the triangular space between the Chancel and the Trinity Chapel. The meeting also resolved to seek a faculty to remove the buttresses at the north-east corner of the Trinity Chapel, 'and so much of the adjoining Wall as will be necessary to make the Public Street there of the Width of Twenty four Feet'.

While the Sexton's House was quickly removed, nothing seems to have been done about the Chapel and on 22nd May 1805 there was another meeting of parishioners to consider whether it should be demolished. It was clearly by then in a poor state of repair, but the meeting opted to provide it with a new gable and a slate roof once part of the north-east corner had been removed. It was also decided to approach the Commissioners for a contribution towards the cost of the work.

32. The mediaeval Trinity Chapel, demolished in 1808.

Again nothing happened until 27th August 1806 when two plans were presented to a further meeting, one for repairing and rounding off the north-east corner of the chapel, the other for taking it down completely and 'palisading' the ground. It was decided to seek estimates for both these alternatives.

Nearly a year later, on 8th July 1807, another meeting decided to rescind the resolution of 22nd May 1805 and to demolish the chapel and rebuild it on a smaller scale to correspond, 'in Breadth and Architecture with the North Aisle of the Church and of the length of the present Chapel'.

By 17th September 1807 Francis Goodwin had 'delineated on Paper' what was proposed, (for which he was paid five guineas), and it was agreed to apply for a faculty to carry out the work and to dedicate some of the site to the road. [14]

In April 1808 William Newham was contracted to take down the chapel and build a new one to the agreed plan. He was paid on account from 10th April 1809 until 10th June 1811 and on 13th June that year his final account was paid, including the sum of £4 4s 0d for 'roof raising'.

The outline of the old chapel can still be seen on the eastern outside wall of the north transept of the church.

33. The rebuilt Trinity Chapel standing to the left of the northern transept of the church.

St. James' Street (Three Pigeon Street in part) (3)

34. St. James' Street, c1910. Coronation celebrations. Note the prominent rounded corners.

The most significant project the Commissioners carried out in this street was the widening of the eastern section alongside what is now Tower Gardens. As already noted, St. James' Street was to become an important part of the new route into the centre of town and, as such, needed widening. The Commissioners, however, shied away from the extensive demolition that would have been necessary in the stretch between Tower Street and the Saturday Market Place, probably on cost grounds, but they had no such reticence when it came to the eastern end.

Before the renaming of 1809 the section of this street east of Tower Street was called St. James' Street and that to the west Three Pigeon Street. There is no obvious record of a survey for Three Pigeon Street, but evidence that the process was applied here is provided by an entry in the Commissioners' minute book of 31st May 1805, requiring an approach to be made to 'Edmund Rolfe Elsden Esqre Mary Brin, Spinster and Richard Watson Owners respectively of Messuages in Three Pigeon Street, the upper rooms of which messuages hang over the foot Pavement, expressing the Desire of the Commissioners that the said upper Rooms should be made perpendicular from the Foot Pavements, or the Lower Parts of such Messuages respectively'. At least two of these properties stood on the northern side at the western end and are now numbered 9 and 11.

The subsequent voluntary improvement is evidenced by a number of brown brick fronts and the prominent rounded corners at the junction with Tower Street/ Tower Place.

For many years the site of the Greyfriars Friary had been owned by the Corporation and leased to various tenants. In 1803, in addition to the tower, there were remains of other buildings, including a gatehouse at the corner of St. James' Street and Tower Place. Built into these ruins were a number of cottages.

In early July 1803 the then tenant, a Mrs. Hamilton, agreed to assign to the Commissioners that part of her lease which related to the land required by them to widen the street and the surveyor was ordered to serve notices to quit on her tenants, with immediate effect. By the end of the month, however, she was refusing to abide by the agreement, but the Commissioners informed her that they were in possession of the land they required and would pay her for it.

35. The mediaeval Greyfriars Gate, demolished in 1806. Wash sketch by the Rev. Edward Edwards.

In fact they already had men on site demolishing the old walls and buildings, a process which seems to have been completed by the end of September. By then the Commissioners had sold a quantity of reclaimed materials including 15,500 bricks (10,000 to the builder Thomas Begley), over 800 tiles, old glass and iron, and a chimney pot. On Christmas Eve that year the Reverend Edward Edwards paid £1 14s for two tons of cobbles from the site. The work was completed shortly thereafter although the Gate does not seem to have been demolished until 1806.

36. The Greyfriars Tower, Lynn as it appeared in 1801. Etching by Robert Dixon. Note the cottages, which were removed for street widening.

Before leaving St. James' Street it is worth considering the circumstances surrounding the building of the theatre, as they were to have dire consequences for the Town Chamberlain, William Newham.

Prior to 1813 the town's theatre was housed in the St. George's Guildhall, but the building was past its best and so in January that year a subscription was started to finance a new theatre. By March the Corporation had become involved, a committee had been formed to run the project and a site had been chosen at the eastern corner of St. James' Street and Tower Place, on the Greyfriars Meadow.

Plans were invited and in May the committee, having considered nine submissions, selected the neo-classical design of architect/builder William Newham, the Town Chamberlain. His only serious rival was Francis Goodwin who had submitted three alternatives, variously priced at £5,230, £4,890 and £4,250. Newham's price was a convenient £4,200.

A contract was quickly drawn up and work began. By January 1814 arrangements were being made for scenery to be painted and for the theatre to be let to John Brunton of London for the ensuing season. [15] In 1815 it opened its doors under the name The Theatre Royal and became part of the Norwich Theatre Circuit.

In June 1815 Newham dropped a bombshell by submitting an account for £6,280, which included £1,653, described as extras. To the committee this was 'totally incorrect and inadmissible' and he was asked to explain himself.

There followed a period of wrangling, with the Corporation offering £5,700 and Newham refusing to budge from his original figure. Finally, in April 1816 the Corporation agreed to pay him £6,100, 'not because it is considered as due to the said William Newham, but to put an end to a business which has occasioned so much trouble and dissatisfaction to the Corporation'.

Newham accepted this sum but the same day he was dismissed from his post as Chamberlain. The Hall Book minute reads; 'The Corporation having taken into consideration the Conduct of Mr. William Newham in the Building of The New Theatre and his General Conduct as Chamberlain, feel they would sacrifice the Interests of the Corporation, if he were continued in office'.[16]

Tower Street (Black Boy Street) (4)

On 6th July 1807 an order was made for Black Boy Street, Sedgeford Lane and Cross Lane to be next paved, flagged and underdrained, but this was because the owners and occupiers desiring the work had subscribed £500 in accordance with the Commissioners' resolution of 28th July 1806. [17] Therefore, Tower Street was not seen as a priority and it seems that no survey was carried out, although the usual gradual refronting did take place.

There was, however, one significant change to the townscape of Tower Street, the completion in 1812 of a substantial neo-classical Wesleyan Chapel, dedicated by the Revd Robert Newton on 13th January 1813.

37. Tower Street, the Rummer Inn, c1920. Rebuilt in brown brick with a rounded corner in 1842.

London Road (The New Road) (5)

The creation of a new road from the South Gate to the eastern end of St. James' Street, to bypass the long established but tortuous route through the Friars, is the most significant single proposal contained in the First Act.

This road is first mentioned on 22nd October 1802, in the minutes of the committee charged with preparing the Bill; 'That a new Entrance be opened into the Town from the Southgate by St. James's Workhouse'. A week later it was resolved that 'the Committee do meet on Wednesday next at Ten o'clock in the Morning at the Gate at the West End of the New Walk to mark out the Line for the proposed new Entrance into the Town…' This was to enable an estimate for the cost of construction to be prepared, subsequently calculated at £676, together with £544 for a new bridge over the Millfleet. The order to construct the road was given on 13th June 1803.

William Walton, a local surveyor, was employed to survey the route, prepare a plan and set out the road, while Charles Dawes was employed to direct and superintend the work. On 16th July 1803 early payments were made to both Walton and Dawes and also to Thomas Bush who was paid £3 9s 4d 'for materials from old Guanock Gates to fill up Ditches etc'.

38. The Old Guanock Gate, demolished in 1803 to provide material to 'fill up ditches etc'. Wash sketch by the Rev. Edward Edwards, c1800.

39. The Norwich Stagecoach at King's Lynn, by James Sillett, 1813. The stage is on London Road about to turn into the widened St. James' Street.

The first entry in the accounts for gravel for the road surface appeared on 29th October 1803 and that for posts and rails for fencing on 21st January 1804, the same day that a man named Woods was paid £252 for work on the new bridge over the Millfleet. The final bills for aspects of construction work were paid on 20th November 1804. By then the new route into the centre was open to traffic.

The only building to fall victim to this process was the Crown Inn, which stood just inside the South Gate, on the eastern side. By 15th September 1803 this building had been demolished for, on that day, the Corporation granted a 50 year lease of much of its site to brewer, Maxey Allen. It was described as 'Ground on which the Public House called The Crown, near the South Gates lately stood ... (except only such Part of the Premises as may be taken by the Commissioners under the Paving Act of Parliament)...'.

The lease was conditional upon him 'building at his own Expence a new House and Offices of at least the Value of Four Hundred Pounds in the room of the old ones lately taken down...' This he did and the new Crown Inn stood on the site until its demolition in 1935.

Evidence that the road had a footway as well as a carriageway is provided by the wording of the notices, which was painted in large Roman letters and placed at both ends of the road. These warned all passengers not to ride or to drive any horses or cattle on the footway adjoining the road 'under the Penalty of the Act'.

The new road was sited on open land between the built up area to the west and the Guanock Bank towards the east. It crossed a mixture of pastureland and market gardens. On 15th October 1804 a committee was set up to estimate the amount of compensation due to owners/occupiers for the land taken. It reported on 5th November 1804 making awards to various owners at the rate of £200 per acre and satisfying others with land exchanges. Money was also paid to owners who had had their land damaged during the construction process.

In 1806 the surface of the road was renewed with gravel from the Hardwick pits and those at South Wootton.

40. The South Gate with the new Crown Inn, c 1810. Watercolour thought to be by James Sillett.

Southgate Street, Friar Street, All Saints Street and Bridge Street (6)

The fact that the Commissioners invested considerable time, effort and money into constructing the New Road did not mean they ignored the old route into town. On 7th May 1804 a committee was appointed to survey these streets and at the same time it was decided that they should be the next to be paved. A week later the surveyor was instructed to make the affected owners aware of what was required.

The record is silent on exactly which properties were affected but these streets contain a number of brown brick fronted buildings, created then or through the follow up process. Two of these are dated, (1806 and 1812).

At the north end of this route stood a bridge over the Millfleet called the Ladybridge. This marked one of the crossover points between the town and South Lynn. In the 14th Century a small chapel dedicated to Our Lady was erected at its north-eastern corner. This enabled travellers setting out to pray and make an offering for a safe journey and for those arriving to give thanks for a journey successfully completed.

After the dissolution this building became the property of the Corporation and in 1569 it was sold to a Mr. Gant. It was subsequently converted into two cottages.

On 2nd May 1792 the Corporation resolved to 'cause a New Arch to be made to Lady Bridge' and 'to be in other parts of it properly repaired…' The western side of this work survives, together with a date stone.

In June 1804 the Commissioners decided to widen the Ladybridge and the old chapel was purchased from George Hawkins, the then owner, for £350. The intention was to demolish the building in order to widen the bridge and also to widen Stonegate Street (then Mill Lane). In addition a public privy was to be erected on the site.

In the event this scheme seemed to have progressed slowly for in February 1806 it was in the list of work yet to be done, described in the following terms; 'Lady Bridge. To enlarge the

41. South Lynn Plain, c1950. Replacement buildings jostle with timber-framed survivors.

42. The Ladybridge Chapel. Wash sketch by the Rev. Edward Edwards, 1803.

bridge 5 feet in width and take down Houses late Hawkins… £70'. Shortly after this fate gave the project a helping hand for William Richards records for 1806 that 'there was a very high tide which demolished the remaining ruins of our Lady's Chapel on the Bridge'. [18]

43. Date stone, 25 All Saints Street.

The scheme was not completed until 1818 when the Commissioners resolved that 'a Sum not exceeding One hundred Pounds be expended in the widening of Lady Bridge, the new Wall or Parapet thereof on the East Side to run in a Line with the corner of Mr. Blackburns House to the Wall already built at the North East Corner of the said Bridge'.

The bridge in its improved state is that depicted on the front cover, but when the Millfleet was filled in, it was no longer needed and with the demolition of the south side of Southgate Street, it is now difficult to visualize a bridge, let alone a chapel, in this locality.

Stonegate Street (Mill Lane) (7)

It is possible that the survey of this street was ordered on 7th May 1804 as part of the general survey of streets and lanes from the White Hart (in St. James' Street) to the South Gate. More likely, it was viewed for improvement when the order for paving was given on 31st October 1808.

It has already been noticed that the western end of this street was widened following the demolition of the Ladybridge Chapel in 1806. By November 1808 works necessary to widen and improve the eastern entrance had been identified and an offer of £31 10s had been made to the affected owner, William Sharpe Foster. Foster refused the offer, stating that he wanted 5 guineas a yard for the ground. The matter was settled in the Quarter Sessions where he was awarded £63 plus £5 costs.

44. Stonegate Street, c1907. The properties on the left were demolished in 1926.

Only part of the northern frontage remains today for the whole of the southern side was demolished in 1926.

Church Street (Red Cow Street) (8)

The survey of Church Street was commissioned on 7th May 1804, and the surveyor was ordered to make the owners aware of the results a week later. At the same time it was agreed to pave the street.

The whole of the eastern frontage has now been demolished but the Commissioners' minutes and old photographs show that the refronting process happened here as elsewhere.

45. 21 Church Street, c1965. A brown brick replacement building.

Nelson Street (Lath Street) (9)

On 5th August 1803 the Commissioners appointed a committee to consider the best way of improving the link between Chequer Street (King Street) and Three Crowns Street (Queen Street) and to carry out a survey of the streets leading from there through Lath Street to Ladybridge.

With so much happening elsewhere in the town it was not until 4th April 1805 that the committee reported on the St. Margaret's Place/Lath Street section, but the Commissioners decided to carry out no more than what was proposed for St. Margaret's Place. The remainder of the report was deferred for future consideration.

By then, of course, the money was running out and the Lath Street scheme was proving controversial. Later that year the opponents of the Bill for the Second Act characterised the Commissioners Lath Street proposals in the following terms; 'they propose (should they obtain the said further tax of 1s.) to lay out and expend £3,000 and upwards in and about the purchase of and pulling down a parcel of old houses in a street called Lath Street, merely to improve the aspect and appearance of the street, the street being in that part of it 26 feet wide, which is 10 feet wider than any one of the public thoroughfare streets in the town, and which expenditure is not at all necessary for the public convenience or usage'. Curiously Chequer Street, double the width of Lath Street at the time, seems to have been overlooked by the protesters.

On 2nd July 1806, shortly after the Second Act gained the Royal Assent, Alderman Self and Mr. Hogg were asked to enquire of the owners of the properties on the north side of the street, at the south end, how much compensation they would require to take down and rebuild part of their property so as to make the street 20 or 22 feet wide. The Mayor was asked to put the same question to the owner of the

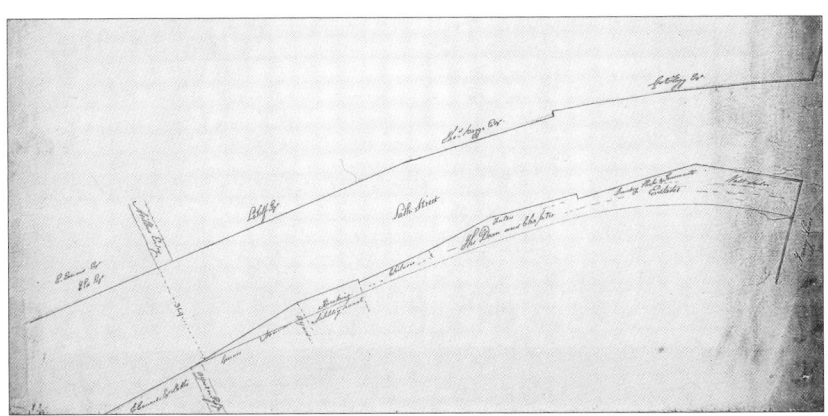

46. Improvement plan for Lath Street, c1806.

47. The Valiant Sailor, Nelson Street, 'the one that got away'.

Valiant Sailor, to facilitate the rounding off of the north-eastern corner of the street by several feet.

Nelson Street is better documented than any of the other streets that the Commissioners improved. Plans must have been prepared for all the streets, but none seem to have survived save for three for Nelson Street. The earliest of these, though undated, seems to have been prepared for the above-mentioned approach.[19] It shows an improvement line at the north-eastern end of the street picking up the line of the churchyard railings and not regaining the then existing street line until opposite Miller's Entry (Devil's Alley). In short it meant the demolition of the Valiant Sailor, a half-timbered mediaeval building, then a public house.[20] The fact that this building is still standing shows that the Commissioners' powers were not unlimited. The problem was that it was largely owned by the Dean and Chapter of Norwich Cathedral as part of the former priory estate. Although not mentioned in the Paving Acts, normal rules seem not to have applied in their case and agreement to demolish seems to have been withheld.

Nothing more is heard of these improvements until 14th May 1810 when another committee was formed to survey the site of the Valiant Sailor following an offer by Alderman Thomas Bagge to sell to the Commissioners the small part of the site he owned.

Again a veil of silence falls until 1st July 1816 when yet another committee was formed 'to examine and report at a future meeting, what alterations are necessary to be made in Nelson Street previous to the same being paved'.

The surveyor was instructed to prepare a new plan, the second of the three to have survived.[21] It shows major alterations at the southern end of the street and a not so onerous improvement line through the Valiant Sailor. The clerk was told to write to the Dean and Chapter, explaining the Commissioners wish to pull down the front of the Valiant Sailor and to ask what compensation was required. Again no mention of such an approach is to be found in the Dean and Chapter records, but it has to be assumed that, if there was one, the answer was no.

At the same time a successful approach was made to Thomas Crane, owner of the house at the

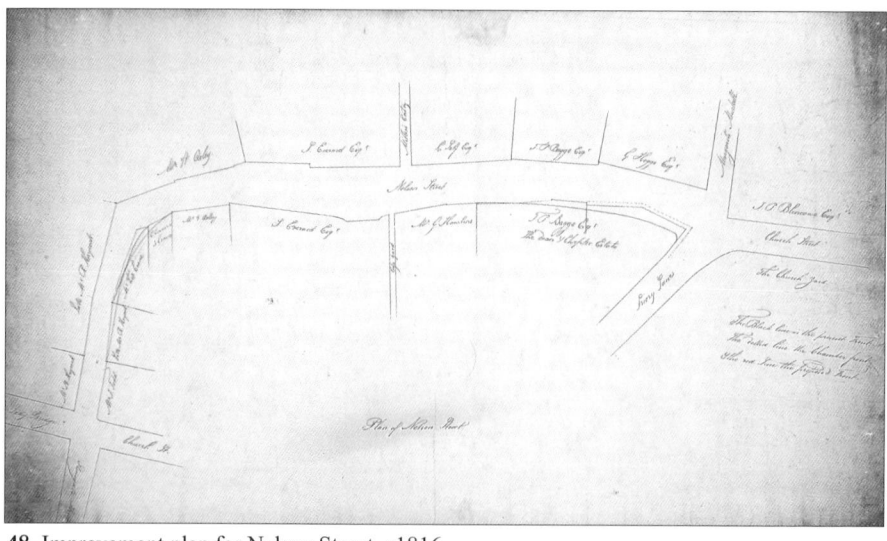

48. Improvement plan for Nelson Street, c1816.

south-west corner of Nelson Street. As a result the improvement at the southern end of the street was carried out. The Three Cranes public house was demolished and the south elevation of what is now Ladybridge House was given a new front onto the cleared land. The improvement was completed with a curved garden wall, which on the inside carries a date stone inscribed WO 1818, referring to the then owner William Oxley, who was paid £150 for the improvement.

49. Nelson Street, looking south, c1905. A view untouched by the Paving Commissioners.

Back to the Valiant Sailor, on 31st March 1817 Alderman Bagge, keen to progress matters, produced a plan showing yet another improvement line through the building. As the plan was not accompanied by an estimate, it was referred to a committee, but nothing seems to have come of this either for on 14 April 1817, the order was given to pave the street. This is the third of the Nelson Street plans and it provides the only evidence that an approach was actually made to the ecclesiastical authorities because, unlike the other two, it is to be found in the records of the Church Commissioners. [22]

No further attempt was made to improve Nelson Street but there were a number of private initiatives in which the Commissioners became involved. In 1832 Thomas Jackson set back part of his house on the west side of the street and was eventually paid £7 10s for ground given up. He evidently built a new counting house on the site for in 1834 the Commissioners were looking into the legality of the waterspouts on the new building.

In 1840 George Todd demolished his house, which stood on the north side of Nelson Street's junction with Church Street. The Commissioners considered the desirability of adding part of the site to the street but with Todd not co-operating they decided the improvement was questionable. The replacement brown brick fronted building on the site has, however, an appropriate rounded corner. Lastly in 1844 Scarlet Everard demolished his stable and coach house together with two adjoining cottages on the east side of the street and erected a gault brick fronted terrace of four houses, described by the Advertiser at the time as 'genteel residences'. [23]

50. Ladybridge House, Nelson Street. Refronted c1817 behind a new curved garden wall dated 1818.

St. Margaret's Place (10)

51. St. Margaret's Place, widened by setting back the churchyard railings in 1805.

As noted above, the committee appointed on 5th August 1803 to deal with the streets from Purfleet Bridge to Ladybridge reported on 4th April 1805, where upon the Commissioners decided to implement only the improvements suggested for St. Margaret's Place.

The main proposal was, 'to widen the Street on the West Side of Saint Margaret's Church Yard by setting back the present West Wall and Palisadoes Eight feet or thereabouts to the East-ward'. This was approved by a meeting of the parishioners and the work was quickly got underway. By the time of the 1806 Plan, it had been completed.

The other improvement agreed in April 1805 was 'the Stopping up (of) the Lane or Passage between the Estate of Thomas Day Esqre and of Mr. Robt Pursglove'.[24] This ran westward from the gate immediately north of the vicarage to the river. In earlier times it had been called Leadenhall Lane, but during the time of the Commissioners was known as Ouse Lane.

If the lane was closed in 1805 it was only a temporary measure for on 17th February 1817 a gate was ordered to be erected at the east end because the lane had become a nuisance owing to the adjoining properties being unoccupied. On 27th November 1820 it was reported to the Commissioners that the lane was a hindrance to the estate to the north and it was ordered to be gated at the western end. Related to this latter closure was the erection of a public privy 'below the Door'.

In 1821 the estate to the south was bought by merchant, Matthew Dawber, who was granted permission to remove the gate at the eastern end. Shortly after this he built a new house adjoining the lane, (the present vicarage).

In 1848 Jacob Jary, the new owner of the premises at the western end, on the north side, asked for the lane to be opened once more ('which Lane had for many years been closed'). The Commissioners did not agree, supposing it would become a nuisance again.

In 1863 the Commissioners themselves decided to investigate the practicality of re-opening the lane but there was opposition, especially from the Mayor, Sir Lewis Whincop Jarvis, as owner of No 2 St. Margaret's Place. He wrote stating his 'determination to resist any attempt to open the East end of

52. House now the Vicarage built shortly after 1821 for merchant Matthew Dawber.

the Lane or to place a Urinal therein'.

The lane was still closed when the Commissioners were disbanded in 1872 but in 1877 the saga was finally brought to a permanent conclusion. In that year the Corporation, as Urban Sanitary Authority, sold the actual ground of Ouse Lane to Jarvis.

In looking at the innocuous black gate today it is difficult to imagine why so much energy was expended on the closure of this little lane.

Voluntary rebuilding in St. Margaret's Place is evidenced by two prominent brown brick fronted buildings, part of number No 1 and the vicarage.

Queen Street (Three Crowns Street) (11)

53. Queen Street, looking south, showing brown brick rebuilding and refronting.

The survey of Three Crowns Street was ordered on 5th August 1803 as part of the general survey of streets from Chequer Street to Lath Street. Perhaps because of its winding nature, the mediaeval properties on the east side were left intact and south of King's Staithe Lane, on the west side, only porches seem to have been removed or, in the case of Clifton House, recessed into the front façade. A number of buildings on that side, however, were subsequently refronted, including No 25, which was refaced in brown brick with red brick detailing. Attached to it is a lead hopper head bearing the date 1812 and the initials G F S, those of the then owner, merchant George Frederick Sayer.

North of King's Staithe Lane, however, there was a considerable amount of remodelling, linked to the need to improve the connection between Chequer Street and Three Crowns Street. The 1806 Plan shows that Three Crowns Street had already been widened on the western side by then, either by rebuilding or refronting.

Until the early 19th century the Ballast Boat public house had stood on the north-eastern corner of Three Crowns Street and King's Staithe Lane. North of it lay the entrance to an L-shaped lane called Little Chequer, the other end of which emerged into Purfleet Place, opposite the Purfleet Bridge.

On 4th April 1805 a small committee was formed 'to consider of the Propriety of stopping up the Lane called Little Chequer and disposing of part of the Ground to Thomas Bagge Esquire'. This resulted in the lane being closed at the Three Crowns Street end. At the same time the Ballast Boat was demolished and replaced with a house. A new Ballast Boat was built immediately to the north of it, incorporating the land of the stopped up lane.

54. 15 Queen Street, built in 1805 following the closure of Little Chequer.

Baker Lane (12)

55. Baker Lane, looking from the High Street, c1900.

It is unclear when Baker Lane was surveyed, but the 1806 list of work yet to be carried out included three entries for it. The front of a house owned by Alexander Smith was to be demolished and rebuilt so as not to project in front of the houses on either side. The side of a house owned by William Turner was to be taken down and rebuilt so as to make the street 13-foot wide at that point. In addition a projection at first floor level (the chamber floor), part of a property owned by the same man, was to be removed and the corner of the related shop rounded. These properties were probably on the south side towards the eastern end. With the rest of Baker Lane they have long since been demolished.

Purfleet Bridge, Purfleet Place (13)

The laying out of the Second New Town, in the 12th century, made no provision for a bridge over the Purfleet to link what later became King Street and Queen Street. Unfortunately these streets abutted opposite sides of the fleet some 100 feet apart. A bridge was subsequently constructed on the King Street alignment but it was only wide enough for foot traffic. It is mentioned in the 1577 survey of the town, is depicted on Henry Bell's drawing of c1675 and was substantially rebuilt in 1782, the evidence for which can still be seen, on the western side.[25]

By the time the need for town improvement was being discussed the limited nature of this bridge had become a major inhibitor to efficient communication along the waterfront and therefore to trade. Accordingly the eradication of this problem became a high priority for both the Commissioners and the Corporation, who had the responsibility for bridge maintenance.

On 20th June 1803 the Commissioners' surveyor was ordered to consider the best way of 'making Communication' between Three Crowns Street and Chequer Street and on 5th August a committee was formed to follow this up. On 26th March 1804 a plan was placed before the Commissioners and the surveyor was ordered to produce estimates. On 3rd December that year the plan was approved with the proviso that the cost to the Commissioners should not exceed £400. The same month the Corporation agreed to match that sum 'being desirous of furthering such a

56. The southern end of Chequer Street (now King Street) before the Purfleet Bridge was widened. Note the soon to be demolished Town Dues Office to the left of the bridge. Watercolour by an unknown artist, c1800.

Plan of General Improvement' and there was also funding from private subscribers such as Thomas Bagge, who donated his share of the £40, paid to him and John Lee for improvement work they had carried out in Page Stair Lane. A nine-man committee, comprising three from each of these groups, was appointed to oversee the work.

The centrepiece of the scheme was the widening of the bridge to enable it to carry four wheeled vehicles. This involved the demolition of the Corporation's Town Dues Office, which stood at the foot of the bridge, on the north-east corner. In addition, on the south side of the bridge, because of the misalignment of the two streets, a building was pulled down 'to add an additional width to the Bridge and to lessen the Angle turning into Queen Street.' Five other properties were also demolished in this vicinity for similar reasons.[26] By January 1806 the scheme had been completed but the cost had exceeded the estimate by a staggering £902 4s 1½d (about 75%).

The Commissioners decided to fund a third of this overspend and in August 1806 the Corporation

57. The Custom House and Purfleet Bridge, October 1874. Watercolour by William Austin.

also agreed to pay a third, raising its contribution to £700 in addition to the loss of the Town Dues Office.

The remainder was to be raised by private subscription, but on 16th November 1807 it was reported that the Purfleet Bridge account still had a deficit of £200 from this source. It was decided that the Commissioners would cover this sum, it being considered that the Corporation had already contributed enough.

Today the bridge stands largely as the Commissioners rebuilt it. The clearance of the buildings to the south effectively removed the northern side of a small east/west street called Wrestlers Street. In 1809 the widened area so created was named Purfleet Place. In 1840 James Fysh employed builder, William Johnson to rebuild houses he owned there, giving them brown brick façades, hence the appearance of Nos 1-3, which look as if they would be more at home on London Road. Surprisingly the Commissioners did not widen the very narrow passageway between Purfleet Place and King's Staithe Square, the primary access to the latter remaining King's Staithe Lane.

58. 1-3 Purfleet Place, rebuilt in 1840 in the 'London Road' style.

Purfleet Street (14)

59. Purfleet Street, looking west, c1910.

It is unclear when the survey of this street took place but it was before February 1806 when the works still needed to be carried out were listed. This list included four entries for Purfleet Street. A property owned by William Laird, was to be taken down and rebuilt in a straight line between the adjoining buildings. Two houses in the ownership of Robert Melvin were to be demolished and rebuilt as per Laird's and the front of a property owned by a Mr. Batterham was to be rebuilt, also in line with Laird's. Finally two houses owned by Mr. Dawes were to be improved. These properties stood in a row on the south side of the street, at its eastern end, close to the High Bridge. Although identified for action it is unclear if they were altered at this time for in 1815 John Laird was paid £90 for the improvement made to the front of his house and the ground given up at the corner of Purfleet Street, and in 1822 it was reported that a house on the south side of the street, owned by Mr. Dawes, was to be pulled down and that it would be desirable for the front to be set back. Voluntary refronting is also recorded but no buildings from the period survive.

King Street (Chequer Street) (15)

The survey of Chequer Street was ordered on 5th August 1803 and the Committee concerned reported its findings to the Commissioners on 20th June 1804. At the same meeting the street was included in a group to be next paved.

Chequer Street was the widest street then existing in the town and consequently little improvement was deemed necessary. By March 1806 only £61 10s had been awarded in compensation for the removal of fronts and the related loss of ground and the smallness of this amount is borne out by the fact that the list of work yet to be done included alterations to the Shakespeare public house, owned by Thomas Allen, at a cost of £73 12s and to the Royal Oak public house, owned by Thomas Bagge, at a cost of £65. Both these timber-framed buildings were subsequently refronted.

The street, however, contains a significant number of brown brick façades. The construction of one of these, in 1827, involved the demolition of a timber-framed building (shown so poignantly in a drawing by the Rev. Edwards) and its replacement for the iron founder, John Aickman.

60. 29 King Street, the former Shakespeare public house, refronted c1806.

61. 19 King Street, before and after redevelopment in 1827. The wash sketch is by the Rev. Edward Edwards.

Another building worthy of mention is the former Plough public house (now No 14). In April 1865 Richard Bagge applied to bring forward the lower front wall of this building 'so as to range with adjoining houses and with the upper storey of the Plough'. This work was carried out in red brick for by then brown brick had almost had its day.

The Tuesday Market Place (16)

By virtue of the square's openness, the buildings fronting the Tuesday Market Place were not deemed to require improvement and accordingly no survey was carried out. The process of rebuilding/refronting in accordance with the prevailing fashion did, however, take place as is evidenced by several façades from the period. This process started just before the passing of the First Act with the remodelling of No 18 for Thomas Bagge by the soon to be Commissioners' surveyor, Samuel Newham.

More dramatic was the change that took place in the centre of the square. When the Commissioners set to work in 1803 the market place was dominated by an elegant Market Cross with associated shambles, designed and erected between 1708-10 by local architect Henry Bell. Unwisely it had been built over a well. By the middle of the 18th century it was clear that part of the building had begun to sink and in 1806 it was shown to be two feet out of perpendicular. In 1825 the associated shambles were taken down and on 23rd July 1829, the Corporation finally decided to demolish the Cross although the order was not carried out until its replacement had opened for business in 1831.

The Market Cross was a lofty structure and its demolition changed the whole character of the square, making it far less inviting except on market days. The function of the Cross and the shambles was moved to a new Market House built by private subscription in 1830, to a design by the Swaffham born architect, William Donthorne. This stood on the west side of the market place, on the site of the Corporation owned Angel Inn. It was in turn replaced in 1854 by the Corn Exchange designed by William Maberley.

62. 18 Tuesday Market Place. The 'Bagge House'. The bow-fronted bay was built in 1803 to a design by Samuel Newham.

63. The Tuesday Market Place with Malam's lamp pillar, c1900.

64. The Tuesday Market Place. Demolition of the lamp pillar in 1925.

For 20 years the square remained devoid of any focal feature but in April 1858 the town was offered a large lamp pillar and water fountain as a gift from the proprietor of the gas works, John Malam. This brings into focus one of the Commissioners' other roles, street lighting. From the outset they contracted out the lighting of a network of oil fuelled street lamps. This arrangement lasted until 1825 when John Malam, of Rochdale, father of the donor of the lamp pillar, secured a contract from the Commissioners to light the town with gas from a 'Gas Manufactory' which he built just outside the South Gate, on part of the Estray Pasture leased to the Paving Commissioners by the Corporation.

The 25-foot lamp pillar confidently carried the date 1858 and Malam was formally thanked for his generosity but it was not erected in the square until early 1861. It was pulled down and sold for scrap in 1925.

The North End (17)

To the Commissioners the North End comprised St. Nicholas Street, St. Ann's Street, North Street and Pilot Street. The works described earlier show that they considered many of the streets of the First New Town, i.e. between the Millfleet and the Purfleet, to be in need of considerable improvement in terms of widening and repaving. North of the Purfleet, however, where the streets were broader and less critical to the town's road network, their approach seems to have been less vigorous. Only one specific improvement is recorded for the North End, the demolition of that part of James Brown's house in Dog Street (North Street), which projected over the street, at a cost of £399 2s.

This lower priority status in the eyes of the Commissioners is further evidenced by the way the paving of the North End was treated. On 28th July 1806, seemingly

65. Date stone.

chastened by the circumstances prompting the need for the Second Act, the Commissioners resolved; 'That where any Inhabitants shall lend to the General Fund Money sufficient to cover the Expence of paving and improving any particular Street or Streets the Commissioners Will give such Street or Streets a Preference in the Order of Paving'.

This provision may well have been triggered by the people of the North End for at the same meeting it was resolved that if they would lend £1,000 to the fund then their streets would be the next to be paved and underdrained. On 4th August it was reported that the money had been subscribed and the work was put in hand.

Like elsewhere, the process of voluntary improvement occurred in the North End and in North Street at least, the Commissioners paid for land given up to the street, but only at half the usual rate.

66. 26 St. Nicholas Street, White's House, built in 1841.

The most obvious survivor from this process is No 26 St. Nicholas Street, rebuilt with brown brick façades and a rounded corner in 1841.

A feature worthy of note at this end of town is the Fisher Bridge. This spanned the original Fisher Fleet at a point where now lies the redundant level crossing of the former Docks Railway. It connected the town with what in 1809 was also called as the North End i.e. 'Row beyond the Fisher Bridge'.

The Corporation had the maintenance responsibility for this bridge and on 30th April 1801 it ordered that 'the Bridge called Fisher Bridge, which is in great Decay be forthwith taken down and rebuilt under The Mayor's Direction and according to a Plan now produced by the Chamberlain'.

The Commissioners, therefore, had no need to consider the bridge for improvement in 1803, but nearly fifty years later the Norfolk Estuary Company decided change was necessary. This organisation was set up to profit from the land reclaimed as a result of forming the Marsh Cut. This new channel from the Lynn waterfront to the Wash changed the outfall of the Fisher Fleet and the approach to the town from the north.

In 1851, the company asked the Corporation for permission to 'alter the present Bridge at Fisher End for the purpose of improving the proposed new Entrance into Town', (from the company's land). The Corporation was supportive and by 27th June 1853 the matter had progressed to such an extent that the company sought permission to completely rebuild the bridge. This was granted and the work was carried out later that year.

67. Demolition of the Fisher Bridge, 1853. Watercolour by William Taylor.

Austin Street (Hopmans Way) and Chapel Street (Black Horse Street) (18)

As an early priority, following the passing of the First Act, the Commissioners carried out a project to improve the connection between Austin Street and Norfolk Street, which at the time was narrow and turned at a right angle. This required the acquisition of land from Robert Pursglove. With the initial offer of £65 being turned down he was served with a notice to the effect that the Commissioners intended to apply to the magistrates for an independent valuation.

68. Austin Street. New link road constructed in 1803.

Carriages'. The work was carried out at a cost of £289 18s 7d.

With this accomplished, on 29th July 1803 a committee was formed to survey Dampgate Street 'and also the Road and Street leading from Little Port Bridge, thro' Hopman's Lane into Black Horse Street...'.

It is unclear if this actually included Chapel Street but it seems likely as the order for the street to be paved and flagged was given on 14th May 1806 and that for Austin Street shortly thereafter.

The record is silent on the nature of the improvements carried out and as both streets have since suffered extensive demolition there is scarcely a building left standing from the period to provide direct evidence although pre-1960s photographs show that rebuilding did take place.

The problem seems to have been solved by 22nd July 1803, however, when the order was given for 'the Line of the New Road leading from Little Port Bridge into Hopman's Lane', to be marked out and for it to be 'opened directly for Passengers and

Norfolk Street (Grassmarket/Dampgate) and Littleport Street (19)

Three years before the Commissioners set to work the Corporation demolished the mediaeval East Gate, which had stood for centuries at the eastern end of Littleport Street. It had long acted as a defensive barrier and a tollgate, but by the end of the 18th century it was in a poor state of repair and the lowness of its arch was proving problematical.

In May 1792 the decision was made to take down the arch on the east side of the Gate and in July 1800 it was ordered that the whole Gate be removed, together with the adjoining houses on the west and south sides. The southern part of the Gate, however, was being used as a public house called the Hob in the Well. In September that year the Corporation leased to Edward Everard part of the site of the demolished Gate on condition that he built 'a New House in the room of the old one lately taken down'. The present public house of that name is the result.

The Paving Commissioners set up a committee on 29th July 1803 'to survey both sides of the Streets leading from the Bridge standing at or near the Place where the Eastgates lately stood to the High Street...' and to agree with the owners and occupiers 'the Removal of such Projections and Incroachments and the purchase of such Property as they (the committee) may deem necessary to be taken or used for the Purpose of widening and improving the aforesaid streets'.

The 1806 Plan shows 12 properties improved in some form or other, and several of these can be identified, but there are many more façades from the period, providing the evidence for subsequent voluntary improvement.

69. Norfolk Street, 1907, showing substantial brown brick rebuilding.

Broad Street, Baxter's Plain and Paradise Lane (Spinner Row) (20)

There is no record of improvement surveys for either Broad Street or Baxter's Plain although the 1806 Plan does show one completed improvement for each and both were new paved shortly thereafter, on the same terms as those that applied to the North End.

On 2nd March 1807 it was made known that 'if a sufficient Sum shall be lent to the Fund by the Inhabitants desirous of the paving and improving the Plain and Broad Street, those Places be next paved flagged and under-drained...'. Within a month £700 had been raised but the subscribers also wanted an improvement to Spinner Lane. To this amount the Commissioners added £200, which was a surplus from the subscription for New Conduit Street and ordered that 'the Plain and Broad Street be next paved flagged and underdrained. And that Spinner Lane be also paved, drained and improved with a new Road (15 feet wide) to be made in a straight Line, with Granite Sides, no Flags or kirb, instead of the present circuitous Road next Aldn Cary's House in his own Occupation (which Improvement the Corporation have consented to). Provided the expenses of Spinners Lane is no more that £312 14s'. In the event half the cost of the improvement of Spinner Lane was paid for by the main beneficiary,

70. Baxter's Plain, the Athenaeum, 1874. Watercolour by William Austin.

Alderman Cary.

The priority project in this area was the widening of Baxter's Bridge, which spanned the Purfleet between Tower Street and Baxter's Plain. On 20th June 1804 the Commissioners approved a plan and estimate for rebuilding this bridge 'upon a more commodious and extensive Scale…'. The 1806 Plan shows that the bridge was widened on its western side.

The most significant change to the appearance of Baxter's Plain took place in 1854 with the opening of the Athenaeum on the site now occupied by the former post office building. The idea of housing the town's literary and scientific societies under one roof was first mooted at a meeting held at the public library in the summer of 1852. A project committee was formed and the site was quickly identified and purchased. Architect William Maberley was engaged to design the building and local builders, James and William Purdy, won the contract for its construction.

The overall cost of the scheme

71. The Cattle market, 1908.

was £6,400, financed by raising debentures, a mortgage on the building and donations, together with rents from the tenants. The building contained two libraries, a museum, rooms for the various societies, including the Lynn Conversazione and Arts Society, and a music hall.

In 1873 this complex was enlarged by the addition of the Blackfriars Hall and the Athenaeum Chambers. The whole complex was demolished in 1936 to make way for the present building.

One of the headline provisions of the First Act was a power given to the Corporation to provide a more convenient site for the Beast Market. To a market town such as Lynn it was important to have a separate site for the buying and selling of livestock but at the time this was carried on in the Tuesday Market Place. It is not difficult to imagine the chaos that ensued every Tuesday when livestock was driven through the town to and from this market especially before the London Road was constructed.

It was not until 1809, however, that the Corporation grasped the nettle by establishing a new Beast Market on land it owned called the Estray Pasture, just outside the South Gate, more or less where the lorry park now stands.

This site served the town for a number of years but in September 1825 representations were made to the Corporation by farmers, graziers and others concerned with the buying and selling of cattle, requesting a new site for this market.

After much discussion, in April 1826 the Corporation agreed to lease to the petitioners, headed by Lord William Bentinck, what was called the Paradise Pasture for use as a Beast of Cattle Market. This site lay between Paradise Lane and Broad Street.

In 1845 the site was enlarged by the relocation of the Framingham's Almshouse to London Road, thus giving the Cattle Market, as it was then called, a more prominent frontage to Broad Street, a position it held until the 1960s when it was relocated to the Hardwick Narrows.

New Conduit Street, Sedgeford Lane, the High Bridge and the Purfleet (21)

72. The Lower Purfleet and the High Bridge looking east, 1864. Charles Bennett's workmen are seen preparing the outfall prior to infilling the fleet.

No improvement survey seems to have been carried out for either New Conduit Street or Sedgeford Lane but both were repaved in 1807. As far as New Conduit Street is concerned a number of

73. Sedgeford Lane, looking west c1900.

private improvements did take place, attracting the usual payments for ground given up, but nothing of this nature is recorded for Sedgeford Lane. Hidden behind these streets was the Purfleet, then an open watercourse. Unlike the Millfleet and the Fisher Fleet, the Purfleet had a substantial number of properties backing on to it, in effect the whole of one side of Purfleet Street, Baker Lane, New Conduit Street, Sedgeford Lane, and North and South Clough Lanes. Large numbers of these properties had projecting privies, which disgorged their unsavoury contents directly into the fleet below, as did the sewers of streets such as Tower Street.

The unpleasant conditions this arrangement created, particularly at low tide, were often graphically described in the local press. In April 1846, in connection with some proposed work to the fleet, the Advertiser commented that it would 'improve the health of the town, as the noxious effluvia constantly arising from an accumulation of filth, in this densely populated district of the place, is any thing but productive of good to the residents there, or the inhabitants at large'.

Some years later the same newspaper reported, 'Faugh! how it smells! The inhabitants of St. John's Terrace and the frequenters of St. John's church have but too frequent occasion to utter this and much stronger exclamations in reference to the open cesspool miscalled a "reservoir", immediately adjacent to that building...'. [27] This referred to the section of the Purfleet, now beneath the Walks, which at that time was acting as a sump for all the sewage swept up from the lower reaches by the tide. Such was this nuisance that the occupiers of the houses had to burn incense to fumigate their properties. Clearly something had to be done.

To guide the debate the Commissioners were informed that the Purfleet 'may be considered as divided into three parts; Upper Purfleet (or Clough Fleet) extending from Baxter's bridge eastward; Middle Purfleet extending from Baxter's bridge to High bridge; and Lower Purfleet, extending from High bridge westward'. The whole fleet was vested in the Corporation, subject to some private rights, including privies, drainage and navigation.

The first improvement took place on the Upper Purfleet. North Clough Lane and South Clough Lane backed onto the Fleet but only in part. The

74. St. John's Church, built in 1846. Print by Thew & Son.

43

remainder to the east, now the site of the swimming pool car park and part of the pool building itself, was clear of structures and builder William Candler was astute enough to spot this as a development opportunity, which could be presented as the removal of a nuisance.

In 1834 he offered to tunnel that part of the fleet and improve the adjacent roadways in return for the site. The Corporation liked the idea and asked Candler to submit a ground plan together with draft elevations of his proposed buildings. Negotiations took place and a deal was thrashed out which included an indemnity against the 'risque of the Tunnel blowing up'. Candler agreed to pay £100 (later reduced to £80) for the contract, which was finalised in January 1835. At the same time the Clough Bridge was altered to line up with the road heading towards it from the south, a scheme the Corporation had been considering for some years.

This improvement did little, however, to improve the overall condition of the Purfleet, the disgraceful state of which continued to provoke strong feelings. It was featured and illustrated in Lee's report on the state of the town's health and in October 1853 the Board of Guardians of the Poor complained to the Corporation that, parts of the Purfleet were an 'intolerable nuisance' and ought to be covered in. [28]

In response the Corporation claimed it had no power to comply with the request.

In August 1857 the owners and occupiers of the properties adjacent to the fleet made a formal complaint to the Corporation. As usual a committee was formed, the report of which was considered in January 1858. The Corporation agreed to fill in the reservoir near St. John's Church provided it was legal to do so. On this the proposal seemed to have foundered for nothing more appears in the Corporation's minutes until November 1862, when the Commissioners drew the Corporation's attention to the state of the Purfleet. This complaint was also sidestepped by referring it to a committee.

In July 1863 the Corporation received a complaint signed by the medical practitioners of the town and the residents adjacent to the Purfleet requesting that immediate steps be taken to remedy the situation and this, at last, set in train the sequence of events which produced the solution to the problem.

Having considered the matter the Corporation invited the Commissioners to make an improvement, as the Purfleet was a 'standing disgrace'. On 5th August 1863 the Commissioners decided to form a committee to co-operate with the Corporation in devising a scheme and shortly afterwards the

75. The Upper Purfleet looking east from Baxter's Bridge, 1864.

76. Demolition of New Conduit Street, 6th May 1865. Drawing by Henry Baines. Note the filled in Purfleet and the High Bridge.

improvement of New Conduit Street, the High Bridge and North Clough Lane. While the Purfleet was being filled in, a group of riparian property owners approached the Commissioners with a view to the improvement of New Conduit Street.

On 5th April 1865 the Commissioners resolved to widen and improve the street by the demolition of some property on the north side and nearly all the property on the south. In May the removal of the High Bridge was added to the scheme and in June it was decided to include an improvement to North Clough Lane by pulling down the north side of that street.

By May 1866 the Commissioners were ready to set out the new street, some 40 feet wide (including pavements) as measured from the remaining north side. This left a sizeable strip of land between the new street and the rear of the properties in Sedgeford Lane, which later that year the Commissioners tried to sell for building, but then decided to plant instead. It remained in this form until the redevelopment of the town centre in the 1960s/70s.

As far as the High Bridge was concerned the surveyor reported on 4th April 1866 that the Borough Treasurer and the Commissioners' Surveyor were instructed to prepare a plan for dealing with the fleet.

It took a further year to iron out the details but by 12th August 1864 the Commissioners and the Corporation were in full agreement on how to proceed and the General Purposes Committee of the former was tasked with carrying out the works, which comprised the tunnelling and filling in of the Purfleet from the west end of the existing Clough Fleet tunnel to the High Bridge. Eight tenders were received and that of Charles Bennett of Lynn was accepted. On 3rd May 1865 the Surveyor reported that Bennett had completed his contract.

As part of this process a certain Peter Pentney took legal proceedings against the Commissioners for the loss of the right of navigation attached to his premises in Sedgeford Lane. In relation to the case the Commissioners arranged for a set of photographs to be taken and on 6th May 1868, it was decided that a duplicate set should be presented to the Lynn Museum. This far-sighted act has enabled us to visualise the offensive state of the Purfleet at that time.

Once the joint working with the Corporation was at an end the Commissioners were able to turn their attention to something that was completely within their powers, the

77. Mediaeval undercroft in Purfleet Street. Sketched by Henry Baines on 30th October 1865 and demolished shortly thereafter.

78. New Conduit Street, looking west c1900.

remaining houses had been taken down and the bridge was being removed. Ten days later the Advertiser carried the following report: ' "HIGH BRIDGE." - The slight elevation in the surface of High street, known by the above lofty designation, is in the course of removal; the pavement has been pulled up and the bridge has been pulled down. In a few days there will have ceased to be anything approaching the semblance of a "hill," the pavement will have been relaid, and the full effect of the Conduit street improvement will be one step nearer realization.'

In conjunction with this work, a property on the south side of Purfleet Street, at the eastern end, was demolished. Within this was a mediaeval undercroft described as measuring 24 feet 6 inches by 20 feet 6 inches and similar to that at Clifton House.

In its report of 17th Jan 1866 the New Conduit Street Committee took great pains to explain that it was 'absolutely necessary to have this structure destroyed, the top of the arch being nearly three feet above the proposed future level of the street'. [29]

Following the removal of the north side of North Clough Lane on 2nd January 1867 the Commissioners named the widened street Blackfriars Street, the name it bears today.

The overall scheme cost in excess of £10,000 and it was the largest single project the Commissioners carried out, and their last.

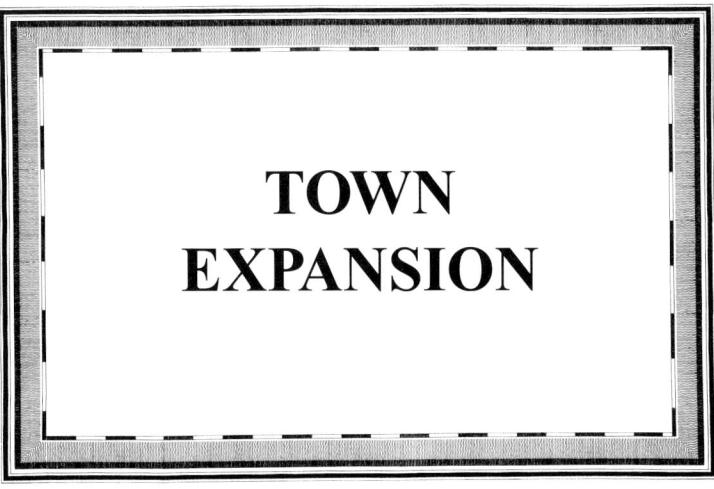

OVERVIEW

The brown brick town expansion of Lynn took place in three broad phases. The first, from 1800 to 1820, was almost wholly devoted to yard building. The second, from 1821 to 1845, was closely related to the construction of the New Road (London Road), the completion of which in 1804 opened up a large tract of land in South Lynn between the built up area and the line of the old town defences. Some advantage was taken of this in the earlier phase, but its development in earnest did not begin until the 1820s. The third phase, from 1846 to 1855, was prompted by the arrival of the railway. As part of the associated infrastructure Railway Road was constructed, linking London Road to Norfolk Street, thereby opening up another tract of land east of the built up area and close to the railway station.

But while the railway triggered a local house building revival, its introduction nationally took away Lynn's trading hinterland and, once the navvies who had excavated the Marsh Cut had left town, the housing market collapsed and this era of town expansion came to an abrupt end.

In all, not counting the yards, 17 new housing areas were created at this time and much of the open land east of the existing built up area was developed.

The quality of this new housing, however, varied greatly, with much of it built as cheaply as possible. It was this cheaper housing, which was swept away as part of the town centre redevelopment and slum clearances of the 1960s. Those at the higher end of the rental market were more substantial, well built and of greater architectural quality. Examples of these are still to be found in Goodwin's Road,

79. St. John's Terrace, 3-5 Blackfriars Road. Built in 1851 by William Salmon Rolin.

London Road, Portland Street, St. John's Terrace and parts of the Everards.

The following sections explain these themes in detail, concluding with a close look at all 17 development areas.

PHASE I 1800-1820

The first national census was taken in 1801. It revealed that in King's Lynn there were some 10,096 people living in 2,012 houses. By the time of the third census in 1821, the town's population had risen to 12,253 and the dwelling stock by 627 to 2,639.

With the exception of London Road, however, Lynn's street pattern in 1820 was much the same as it had been at the start of the century. This apparent contradiction is explained by the fact that the townsmen had utilised one of the simplest forms of development to satisfy the demand for new housing, 'the yard'. [30] The yard was essentially a small group or row of houses built to the rear of a property fronting a public street and usually accessed via an arched opening from that street. As there was no need to buy land or construct streets, it was an inexpensive and therefore popular form of investment for the owners of the frontage properties, especially when the demand, as in this case, came from the lower end of the social scale.

Yards existed in the town prior to the 19th century but seemingly not in any great numbers. Early maps are too stylistic to pick them out with any degree of certainty but Newham's 1806 Plan is in sufficient detail to speculate on the presence of at least 14 and no doubt there were more.

80. Law's Yard in Bridge Street, demolished in 1912. Note the mansard roof.

The majority, however, were created in the early 19th century. The evidence for this is provided by a variety of sources. William Richards, after doubting the accuracy of the 1801 and 1811 census figures and speculating that the one for 1801 must in reality have been higher because of the 'great and unusual number of untenanted houses found in different parts of the town in 1810, amounting in all to above one hundred', went on to have second thoughts through observing 'that a still greater number of new houses, of a smaller rent, had lately sprung up in certain alleys and outskirts of the town, and all tenanted, ...', in other words, the yards. [31]

Being sub-standard from the start the yards were demolished in the 1930s, but photographic evidence shows that most yard houses sported the roof dividing firebreak party walls brought in as a regulatory measure by the Second Act. In addition, the pantiled mansard roof, so characteristic of many of the yard houses, was also a feature of those yards built off Providence Street, around 1806, suggesting that the two were broadly contemporary.

A perusal of the yard names also confirms their date. The majority were derived from the surnames of the shopkeepers and tradesmen who occupied the associated premises fronting the public streets and many of these appear in White's Directory of 1836. [32]

It was also about then that the first comprehensive listing of the yards was published. In all there were 159 at that time containing 962 houses in which lived around 4,500 people. [33] Norfolk Street had the most, 29; Pilot Street had 14, the High Street 12, Jews Lane 10, North Street 8, with King Street and Queen Street having 6 each. In fact all the main streets had their yards.

That the yards were built for the families of unskilled working men (a group swelled by the labourers brought in to dig the Eau Brink Cut), is borne out by the early trade directories. Of all the people living in the yards in 1836 only one was considered of sufficient status to warrant an entry in White's Directory of that year, Samuel Hye, a blacksmith, who was to be found in Crown Yard.

Further evidence, if any was needed, that the yards were a method of creating cheap housing to let to the unskilled is provided by their annual rental value. The Boundaries Report lists the average rents for all the houses in the town's streets and yards. Those for the yards cluster at the bottom end of the range with 629 of the 962 yard houses attracting as little as £3 - £6 per annum compared with Tower Street at £12 16s 5½d, Norfolk Street at £17 5s 9¼d, Queen Street at £21 11s 1d, King Street at £39 16s

81. House on the north side of Valinger's Road, dated 1807.

0d and Tuesday Market Place at £50 0s 6d.

With the yards soaking up the demand for new housing, it is not surprising that landowners and developers were slow to take up the opportunities presented by the laying out of the New Road from the Southgate to the Millfleet and the improvement of the existing road from there to the Purfleet. This project opened up a large tract of land and the increased value this generated was highlighted by the opponents of the Second Act, [34] but nearly all the landowners who benefited from this potential windfall seemed content merely to pocket the compensation they received for the loss of their land to the road.

The exception was William Smith, the devisee of the will of Robert Dixon. Dixon died in 1801 leaving a piece of garden ground in South Lynn, between the lanes which were to become Valinger's Road and Providence Street. Smith, who has already been featured in relation to the Wenn's building, was required to sell the Garden for the benefit of Dixon's relatives so, when in 1804, the land was given a frontage to the New Road, he grasped the opportunity this presented. Dividing the land into several parcels, he sold them for development in 1806/7 and, as a result, several houses were built on all three road frontages. At the same time a number of yards were built on the backland.

No other house building took place on the London Road land at this time and these early houses were to remain in splendid isolation for the best part of 15 years before town expansion really took off. Armes commented that only three houses existed along the entire length of London Road at this time. [35]

PHASE II 1821 – 1845

After the period of uncertainty that characterised the aftermath of the Napoleonic Wars, the opening of the Eau Brink Cut and the Cut Bridge in 1821, together with the Coronation of George IV that same year, combined to produce an air of optimism in the town. This soon expressed itself in the bricks and mortar of a speculative house-building boom.

The main focus of this activity was London Road and the land it had opened up earlier. The first man to start building was John Abraham. In 1821, he bought a piece of pastureland on the Millfleet to the west of the Jewish Cemetery. On this he built a mixture of houses and called his development Coronation Square.

Shortly after this, building recommenced on the London Road frontage. On the east side, between what is now Windsor Road and Guanock Place,

82. View of Lynn from the Cut Bridge, 1840. Drawn by James P Hunter.

83. South Street looking east, c1965.

William Newham and others erected a range of two and three storeyed houses. The frontage from there to Hospital Walk was also built at this time, some of it on land owned by seedsman, Thomas Marshall, whose market gardens were to provide a number of sites for housing development in the coming years. [36]

At its northern end, south of the Millfleet, London Road had cut across a field owned by the Ffolkes family of Hillington Hall. This stretched as far west as the vicarage garden and Vicarage Lane, adjoining Coronation Square. In 1823, or thereabouts, this land was sold to merchant, William Ayre, who proceeded to dispose of frontage plots on London Road, singly and in groups. Two terraces were the result, behind which, on the western side, Ayre himself developed Millfleet Terrace, Hillington Square and Hillington Row. [37]

Back at the southern end of London Road, in 1825, there was a determined effort to provide the town with a prestigious modern entrance by the construction of two substantial terraces each three storeys high and of a uniform design. On the western side, on what was known at the Quaker's Ground, James Gathergood started Buckingham Terrace but before he had got very far he died leaving Edmund Trundle to complete the work.

On the opposite side, Charles Goodwin developed Guanock Place, together with the less grand Guanock Terrace and Guanock Row, on land bought from the Corporation. It was to be the first of four areas he was to develop. [38]

It is worth noting that this was the only piece of land from the Corporation's extensive land holding to be sold for housing. This reluctance on the part of the Corporation to dispose of its land for development was to have a marked effect on the form and character of this part of town.

By 1830 the development of London Road was largely complete, enabling William White, in 1836, to describe it as a 'broad and spacious street ... lined with handsome modern houses'.

Two other housing areas were started at this time, Cade's Garden and Highgate, both catering for the lower end of the rental market. The first of these, which ultimately comprised South Street and Wood Street, was built on land sold to John Palmer in 1823. Building at Highgate, which lay just outside the Borough boundary, in the Parish of Gaywood, was begun around 1825.

By the time of the 1831 Census the town's population had risen to 13,370, an increase of 1,117 since 1821. Over the same period the housing stock had increased by 275. In Gaywood the population had risen from 474 to 924, largely as a result of the development of Highgate and Albion Place.

That the developers tried to cater for a more affluent tenant than those in the yards is shown by the annual rental values of some of the new housing. Around 1835, the value of the 27 properties in Coronation Square averaged £12 1s 2d, the 106 in London Road, (including Buckingham Terrace), produced an average of £14 8s 2¼d and the 25 houses in Hillington Square could be rented for £10 10s 0d, double or treble what was being achieved in

84. Buckingham Terrace, London Road, from the north.

the yards.[39] This observation is reinforced by the 1836 Directory entries, which show these developments to be occupied by large numbers of people of independent means and those pursuing middle class professions.

The decade between the Censuses of 1831 and 1841 saw acceleration in the pace of development, but the houses built were generally more modest than those of the previous decade.

In 1830 Richard Checker and Lewis Weston Jarvis bought a market garden stretching from London Road to Friars Street and developed Checker Street. [40] Around this time work also started on Kirby Street, off the south side of Norfolk Street. The land developed was part of the second of Thomas Marshall's market gardens to be made available.

In 1831 Union Street was laid out to link Coronation Square with All Saints Street. Two years later, Richard Checker, spurred on by the success of the street bearing his name, bought a piece of land to the south of Windsor Road and laid out Windsor Row. Alongside this the same year William Richardson started to extend Garden Row.

In 1834 Thomas Marshall released the next section of his Windsor Road garden to William Triance, who developed Keppel Street and Victoria Street. In 1836 William Candler teamed up with John Southwell to buy a substantial tract of land in the Clough Garden, but they soon ran into financial difficulties and sold the majority of it to Charles Goodwin. Between the three of them they developed Melbourne Street, Bentinck Street, and Russell Place. In 1839 Charles Goodwin bought the remaining available piece of this field and developed Regent Street.

Finally in this decade the last major landowner on the London Road frontage, Edward Everard, decided to develop his land. In 1837 he laid out streets and began selling off parcels of land for house building. These streets became North Everard Street, South Everard Street and St. John's Street.

In 1841 the Census showed that the town's population had risen by 2,669 to 16,039 and the housing stock had increased by 582 to stand at 3,496, with again most of the increase in South Lynn. At this time several of the key players in this phase of town expansion were to be found living on London Road. [41]

In the previous 20 years Lynn had experienced house building at an unprecedented rate, with several developments in the course of construction

85. 23-25 North Everard Street, looking west. These houses have good quality architectural detailing.

at any given time, but over the next five years this rapidly tailed off until in 1845 scarcely a house was being built. There were some small additions to existing areas in that time, notably off Windsor Road and Valinger's Road, but only one man had the confidence to continue developing and that was Charles Goodwin.

Goodwin had completed his Guanock Field development in the 1820s and his Clough Garden site in the 1830s. In 1840 he bought an orchard from Thomas Marshall and laid out Albert Street, connecting Austin Street to Norfolk Street, but, just prior to this, he embarked on a project to create a complete new garden suburb. This he called Goodwin's Fields, a development that pre-dated the garden city and garden suburb movement by some 50 years. Work commenced in 1842 with the construction of the road, which later became Goodwin's Road.

86. Burnet's Plan of King's Lynn, 1846. It shows the Phase I and II town expansion and the newly built railway station.

PHASE III 1846-1855

87. The Paragon of Lynn, 1828. On such vessels Lynn's prosperity depended.

For centuries Lynn's position as a major distribution centre, dispatching imported goods via the internal waterway system to a large part of the country and exporting by sea the produce from much the same area, went largely unchallenged. To the town's merchants this must have seemed like the natural order of things, then came the railways, Lynn lost its trading hinterland and went into sharp decline.

In later years when men who had witnessed these events penned their memoirs, all understood what had caused this dramatic change in Lynn's fortunes. Local bookseller, John Aitkin, spoke for them all when in 1866 he wrote; 'It is probable that few towns have suffered more from the general introduction of Railways than Lynn'.[42] At the time, however, this bleak future was not seen as a foregone conclusion and the efforts made to improve the town's trading position served to mislead to such an extent that there was an ill-judged upsurge in house building.

The great railway mania took place in 1844-5 and the business community of Lynn was eager to take part in the misguided belief that this would actually expand the town's hinterland. In 1846 schoolmaster William Burnet wrote, 'A Bill, or rather, two Bills have passed the legislature, the one to extend a Railway between Lynn and Dereham, and the other between Lynn and Ely. The latter will connect the town with the Midland Counties, and will consequently open up a new source of trade that may be turned to immense advantage, and as the works on that line are in full progress, the time is not far distant when Lynn will be the Port for Birmingham'.

He also commented on the perennial concern of Lynn's merchants, the condition of the port, which he considered to be 'in a ruinous state…, the channel by which it is approached, is long, intricate, and filling up with silt…' but 'Another Bill is now before the House of Commons, for cutting a new, and a *deeper* out-let for the waters of the *Ouse*,…'.

Drawing these two themes together he concluded; 'Within the last year, *a great augmentation in the commerce of Lynn appears to have taken place*! but that augmentation is merely the effect of the importation of material for the construction of the railways now in progress in its vicinity; that augmentation therefore, is but temporary. We must look to other sources for our future commercial prosperity, and when our *Railways* are completed, and the *new entrance to the port from the sea* is effected, we feel *sure* that, in the hands of honourable and enterprising merchants, *the trade of Lynn must increase*!' [43]

In the event the rail link came first. Its most active promoter was John Williams, a solicitor in partnership with Charles Goodwin, and Frederick Partridge. Williams saw this largely as an opportunity to make a personal fortune and in April 1844 he was responsible for issuing the prospectus for the Lynn and Ely line, and in the following September, that for the Lynn and Dereham line. Plans were drawn up for both and for the Lynn station.

The promoters wanted to site the station as close to the centre of the town as possible so they chose a route, which brought the line in north of the Purfleet, almost as far as the cattle market. Having breached the mediaeval town wall, the intention was to close the Echo Road (Blackfriars Road) and construct a new road further west, which would link London Road to Norfolk Street. The station was to be sited on the eastern frontage of this new road. Two owners held the majority of the land required, the Corporation and Edward Bagge.

In March 1846 the contract for constructing the first phase of the Lynn - Ely Railway was awarded to William Smith Simpson and the line was opened the following October. [44] The station building was constructed by John Sugars and was described as temporary because, for some reason, it was not built on the new street but against the Echo Road, just north of the present railway station. [45]

As for the other great project, the Marsh Cut, progress was not quite so straightforward. The Act mentioned by Burnet received the Royal Assent on 18th August 1846, but there was little support for its grandiose provisions and so it was amended in 1849, enabling the Corporation and the Eau Brink Commissioners to contribute funds.

A year later the Norfolk Estuary Company entered into a contract with Messrs Peto and Betts to carry out the necessary work and the cutting of the first sod took place on the West Lynn side on 8th November 1850. Unfortunately, in August 1852, an injunction was taken out by the Eau Brink Commissioners to stop the work because of the method being used to create the channel. It took a chancery suit and a new Act (9th May 1853) to get the work started again. In October 1853 the first ships passed through the new channel and in November the old channel was closed.

The main reason these major changes provoked a resurgence in speculative house building was the arrival of large numbers of navvies to construct these projects. This stimulated demand for accommodation, although those associated with the railway do not seem to have produced a spate of new house building, probably because there was sufficient slack in the existing

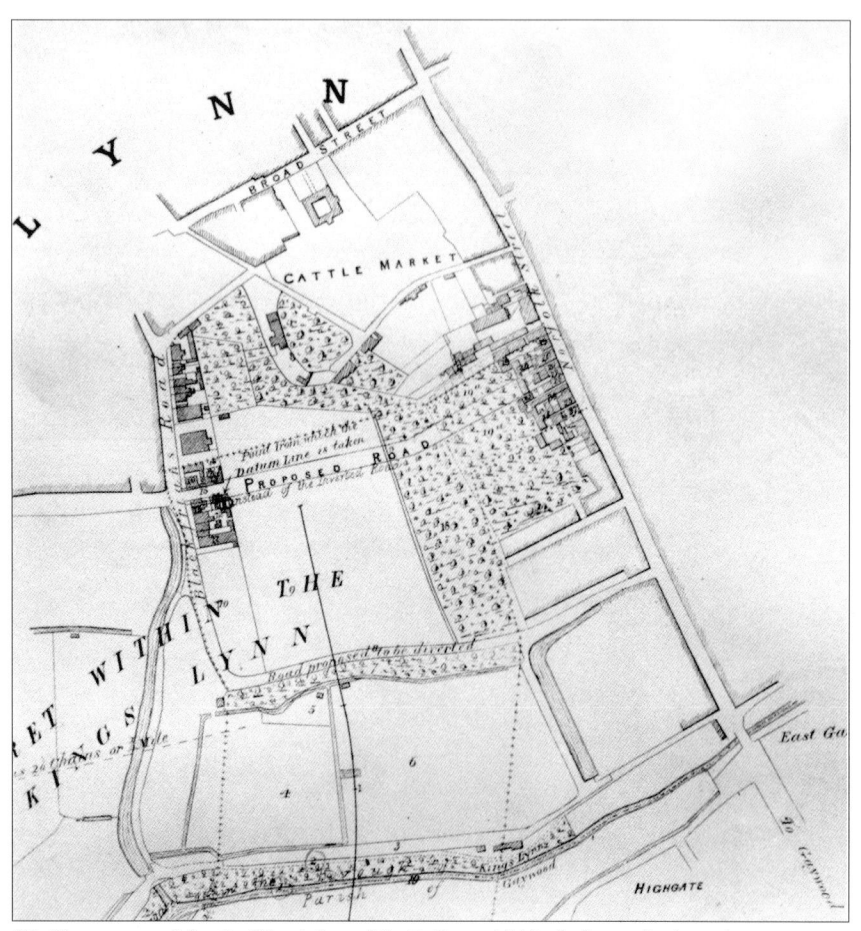

88. Plan prepared for the King's Lynn/Ely Railway, 1844. It shows the intention to terminate the line on Railway Road.

market to accommodate them.

In addition the arrival of the railway station, with the expectation that people would want to live nearby, provided the impetus for the development of the Blackfriars Pasture.

In the event this new era of house building started slowly. On 24th April 1847, under the headline 'IMPROVEMENTS', the Advertiser released land, which was surplus to railway requirements, and on this William Smith Simpson built Portland Street and Henry Barnett laid out Wellesley Street and Waterloo Street.

On 25th August 1849 the Advertiser reported that; 'A large number of houses are now in course of erection, in the field opposite to the station, in which place a complete town will shortly spring up. The

89. Tuesday Market Place, 8th November 1850. The procession is on its way to witness the cutting of the first sod of the Marsh Cut.

commented; 'In looking round the neighbourhood of the terminus, we are surprised that individuals possessing property contiguous thereto, do not seem to make an effort to turn it to some account - as there is much scope for enterprize on the part of active proprietors. This locality must become eventually a place of great bustle, and in a few years from this time, any projected plan in this early stage would soon repay itself a hundred fold. Already some excellent dwellings are erected in the Railway Street, and from their position, they must always be valuable property. It is now we believe, tolerably certain, that the permanent terminus will be commenced this summer,...'.

Things started to pick up elsewhere, however, when John Keed, bought the last remaining piece of the Clough Garden and started developing Whincop Street and Whincop Place.

In 1849 the East Anglian Railway Company, the successor to the Lynn related companies, decided to abandon plans for a permanent station. This streets seem to be laid out most judiciously, and some of the buildings are intended for residences, that seem to be much wanted in this place'.

Originally the Bagge family owned the whole of the Blackfriars Pasture and whilst they had sold a substantial part of it to the railway company they had retained the piece to the west of Railway Road and the frontage to the southern section of Blackfriars Road. In 1850, on the former, Richard Bagge laid out Market Street and Albion Street and sold the latter strip to William Salmon Rolin who, in 1850, started to build the elegant St. John's Terrace. [46]

By 1850 the activity near the railway station had stimulated fresh phases of development on several of the housing sites started earlier. Following the demolition of the South Lynn vicarage, John Nurse Chadwick, bought the site and developed Chadwick Street. On Marshall's Garden, north of Windsor Road, the final phase of the development was commenced with the construction of Wellington Street. In Highgate a western frontage was added to Front Row and on Kirby's Ground the remainder of the site was sold to William Lawrence, who developed Marshall Street, Stanley Street and Bedford Street.

The following year William Salmon Rolin started to develop the old brickyard in Exton's Road and Robert Mott and others bought a piece of land to the north of the railway station and started the development which became known as Lower Canada.

Between 1841 and 1851 the town's population rose by 3,316 to 19,355 and the housing stock increased by 549, including 54 houses, which were in the course of construction. Building continued apace and in the next few years a further 80 houses were built but when in 1853 the navvies working on the Marsh Cut left town, the bubble burst and the housing market crashed leaving a number of bankruptcies in its wake.

Some years later, John James Coulton, who was the Superintendent Registrar at the time, summed up these circumstances as follows; '…the population (of the town) advanced steadily and rapidly up to 1851, but lost during the next ten years rather more than it had gained during the preceding ten, and that in 1871 it was only 324 more than it was in 1841, thirty years before. The increase from 1841 to 1851 was owing to the railway and Estuary works which brought a great influx of population, for whom houses were needed, and persons engaged in the building trade were attracted accordingly. The reaction was such that at one time about 800 houses were unoccupied, and in 1871 four only were being built, two of which were never finished, and were afterwards taken down. The depression in house property arose, not only from the discontinuance of the works, which had attracted population, but from the effect of the railway system on the trade of the town and port, which for a time was very injurious'. [47]

Thus ended the brown brick era of town expansion, a period which had had a dramatic impact on the town, more than doubling its housing stock between 1801 and 1861. When house building picked up again later in the 19th Century, the new developments were sited outside the old town and built of imported bricks, brought in by rail.

Before looking at the nature of these new developments, it will prove instructive to consider the career of one of the builders from this phase, William Salmon Rolin.

Rolin was born in Lynn in 1820, the son of Daniel Rolin, a shoemaker, and his wife Ann. He is listed in the 1841 census as a joiner's apprentice, at home with his parents in Chapel Street. In 1845 he married Mary Ann Andrews at St. Nicholas Chapel, although he was recorded as living in Edmonton, Middlesex at the time, suggesting he was working there.

By 1847 he had a house in Broad Street and had set himself up as a builder. On 13th May 1848 the Advertiser reported, under the headline THE NEW ALMSHOUSES, OR FRAMINGHAM'S HOSPITAL, 'We understand that the contracts for those buildings have been opened and that of Mr. Rolin, builder of this town, has accepted. The amount of Mr. Rolin's contract was £1,730 10s. It is only within the last year of two that this gentleman

90. The South Lynn Vicarage, demolished in 1850. Etching by William Taylor.

91. The Framingham Almshouses, built by William Salmon Rolin in 1848.

commenced business here, and as the work in question is of a public character, it will tend, if properly done (and of this we have no doubt), to establish his reputation'.

That it did is shown by the 1851 census which records him as a builder employing 14 carpenters, 4 bricklayers, 1 house mason, 6 brickmakers and 10 labourers; no mean workforce for a man so recently established.

If additional proof of Rolin's abilities was necessary one need look no further than Lee's Public Health Inquiry of 1852. Rolin gave evidence on the state of the town's streets, drainage and water supply and was described in the report as 'a very intelligent builder'. [48]

In his submissions Rolin stated that he was the owner of 'about 50 houses in Lynn', reflecting the fact that he had been very active, building in Wood Street, North Everard Street, Exton's Road and St. John's Terrace. [49] In 1852 he moved into the house he had built for himself at the eastern end of that terrace (now the Belgrave Hotel). At the age of 32 William Salmon Rolin had well and truly arrived.

Given his drive and self-confidence it will come as no surprise to learn that he was frequently in dispute with the Corporation and the Paving Commissioners. He also successfully sued the East of England Banking Company over the way his finances were being managed. In 1853, no doubt thinking he could do a better job than the existing councillors, he stood for election and managed to produce a late rally to squeeze in by two votes. He seems, however, to have been overlooked by the corporate body, although he did have the support of John Sugars, who seems to have treated him as something of a protégé. In 1854 Rolin was elected a Guardian of the Poor.

Emboldened by this success he decided to branch out. On 13th November 1852 the Advertiser carried the story of the reopening of a shipyard near the South Gate, commenting that, 'Mr.. Rolin, the builder, has laid down a vessel of between 400 and 500 tons register, which he intends to complete with all possible speed, and as far as practicable, to extend this department of his business'.

So Rolin the builder had become Rolin the shipbuilder and ship owner. In August 1853 it was reported that five of the crew of his ship, the Egypt, had died of fever near Demerara. Later that year the Young England was launched from his yard, followed by the Macedonia and, in September 1854, the Alberta.

Rolin's meteoric rise, of course, was financed by borrowing secured against his property, which, while the rents were being paid, was fine. Unfortunately for him when the market crashed he fell with it.

92. Launch of the Arethusa on the River Nar. Sketch by Henry Baines.

On 28th October 1854 the London Court of Bankruptcy held its first meeting re the bankruptcy of William Salmon Rolin and Thomas Bateley Rolin. The meeting was told that one of the bankrupts was at the time in Australia and the other was supposed to be abroad. It transpired that William Armes had brought the whole shaky edifice crashing down, petitioning over a debt of £363. 14s. 11d. Total debts, once assets had been sold, were eventually calculated at over £2,300.

A further meeting in December was informed that Thomas Bateley Rolin (Rolin's younger brother) had left England to look after the partnership's vessels in Australia, while Rolin himself, who had been pronounced an outlaw, had absconded to Hull some three months earlier and had not been heard of since.

Rolin, of course, was a larger than life character whose shipping venture was as much to blame for his downfall as the housing slump, but the essence of his story applied to many other men who had speculated in the housing market at this time.

THE ANATOMY OF EXPANSION

The Building Process

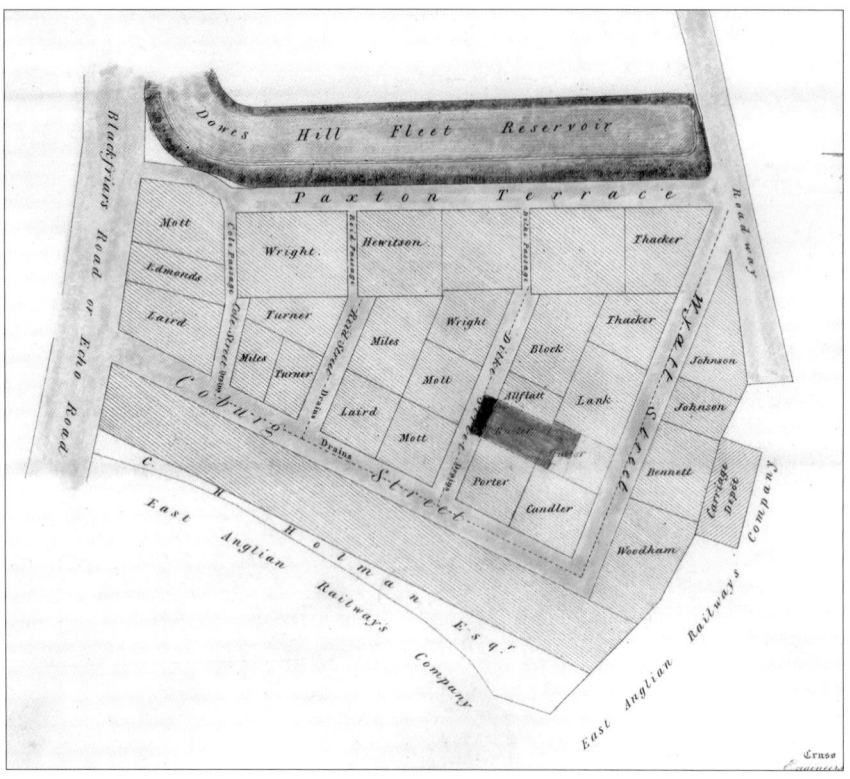

93. Plan prepared in August 1851 by Cruso & Maberley showing the street and plot layout for the development of Lower Canada.

In the 19th century there was no system of town and country planning, no local authority assessing the need or demand for housing and preparing development plans setting out land allocations. Virtually all new housing was produced for rent on a speculative basis, on sites promoted by landowners and developers.

In Lynn, however, the situation was not totally random for the construction of the London Road and Railway Road (the first sections of the old town relief road) guided most of the expansion to the very locations a modern town planner would have chosen, given the circumstances that prevailed at the time.

The process started with the landowner. He could either develop the land himself or sell the site, to someone wanting to develop. Most took the latter course with the notable exception of Edward Everard who, no doubt through an agent, developed the area bearing his name. Most land was sold freehold although the Ffolkes family and the Quakers preferred to sell on long building leases.

It was for the developer to decide how best to lay out the streets, but if he ultimately wanted the Paving Commissioners to assume responsibility for their maintenance, he would be mindful of the fact that they needed to be through routes not what in today's terminology would be termed culs-de-sac.

Once the street pattern had been determined the land would be sub-divided into blocks for sale, either directly to builders or to investors who would employ a builder to construct the houses for them. The houses when built would either be put up for sale en bloc as an investment or individually rented out. This part of the process is well illustrated by the plan prepared in 1851 for the development of Lower Canada.

No development was possible without the 'money men' who provided the mortgage finance to buy the land and build the houses. These included the town's bankers some of whom, like Everard and Jarvis, were also developers. Title deeds, however, make it clear that smaller investors provided much of the money. Most builders financed their work in this way with the inevitable consequence that when there was a sudden slump in the market, many found themselves in difficulties.

Turning now to the method of building nearly all the houses were built in terraces, but not as they would be today from foundation to roof in one operation. In fact very few of the Lynn terraces were wholly built by one builder, the exceptions being Buckingham Terrace (almost), St. John's Terrace, the terraces in Portland Street and those on the Guanock Field. Evidence from the first two show that even these were built as a series of individual dwellings, or in small groups, which eventually linked up to form a terrace, with no discernible joins. In this way each house could be let as soon as it was dry enough to be lived in.

Most street terraces were an amalgam of houses built in blocks of three to six by different builders. It was for the developers to ensure that these blocks

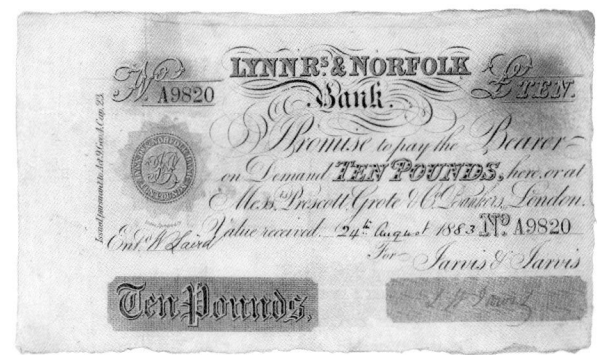

95. A ten-pound note issued by the Lynn & Norfolk Bank (Jarvis & Jarvis) in 1883.

knitted together and the brickwork at the end of each was deliberately left toothed to enable this to happen. Here too, it is often difficult to spot the join but each builder tended to leave his mark in the detailing, the obvious signature features being door cases and fanlights. It is by these that the individual blocks can be identified.

There were also other forces in play to ensure that the developments were broadly homogenous, safe and relatively pleasant to live in, subject of course, to the public health problems of the day. The building regulations contained in the Paving Acts, as described in the first part of the book, also applied to this new house building, although enforcement was patchy and the Commissioners' minutes contain a steady stream of cases of non-compliance by builders.

The other main source of control was the requirements placed on developers by landowners and on builders by developers in the form of covenants in the sale documentation. Often a building line would be specified, as was the case on Railway Road where Richard Bagge stipulated that, 'the front of each dwelling house shall face the Street and be placed exactly upon the Line now staked out...'. [50] Variations on this theme required houses to be built a certain distance away from the street. In selling land to William Candler, between North and South Clough Lanes, the Corporation was even more specific. He had to build, 'in one uniform line or range and make each Tenement or Dwellinghouse of the same height from the Surface...' [51]

Sometimes a minimum sum of money to be spent on a development would be subject to a covenant, such as the £3,000 the Quakers required Trundle to outlay on Buckingham Terrace and the

94. Cross Lane c1934. A pair of cottages showing toothed brickwork awaiting construction of the next cottage.

£500 James and William Purdy had to spend on six houses in Stanley Street. It is also clear that the Quakers specified the standard of facilities to be installed in the houses in Buckingham Terrace.

A restriction on projections into the street was a common requirement where there was to be no front garden. This was the case in North Everard Street where Rolin was told that, 'no steps windows or projections (except the cornices) shall be made built or placed in the front of any house… so as to extend or overhang beyond the Ground line of … North Everard Street and that no gate nor door shall be made to open outwardly into the … street'.[52] Similar restrictions were placed on builders by Richard Bagge in Railway Road.

In respect of the amenity of the tenants a variety of restrictions were included in the documentation. On Goodwin's Fields there was to be no brick making. This also applied to Lower Canada, with the addition of tile making, lime burning and bone burning. On the Everards there were to be no blacksmiths' shops nor any buildings in which were carried on any noisome or offensive trade. The latter also applied to Albert Street, Goodwin's Fields and Lower Canada. On Albert Street there was also a prohibition on steam engines and gas manufacturing, but then this site was very close to the house of the development's promoter, Charles Goodwin.

The Architecture

The main elements of the architectural style of the period were outlined earlier. These can be summarised as Georgian, built in brown brick with rounded corners. This description also applied to the town expansion housing but such was its volume that trends in detailing are more obvious and therefore can more easily be analysed.

Starting at the top, roofs generally slope down to external guttering but some parapets exist, especially in London Road. These are mostly plain but a number of decorative examples are to be seen in the Everards, Portland Street and Railway Road. All roofs display the firebreak projections required by the Paving Acts.

96. House in Guanock Place, built c1826. A typical Phase II elevation.

97. 97 London Road. Elaborate door case and fanlight of 1830.

98. House in Marshall Street built in 1851. It shows the basic house type of Phase III.

The style of decoration used as embellishment differs between the phases. In Phase II, with some notable exceptions, door openings do not have doorcases but are arched in a semi-circular form to provide a space for a decorative fanlight, of which 12 different types can be identified. Some buildings of Phase I and the early part of Phase II feature red brick skewback arches above the window openings as a continuation of an 18th Century style element.

The other prominent decorative feature is the plat band, a raised horizontal strip of stuccoed brickwork, which is usually positioned immediately beneath the sills of the first floor windows across the whole width of a building or terrace. These are usually plain but in London Road, notably on the work of John Sugars, they are highly decorative, sporting a palmette design incorporating either acanthus leaves or tulips.

In Phase III, the decorative aspects of some of the low rental houses stayed much the same as those of the earlier phases, although the fan shaped fanlights acquired a solid filling. The higher rental properties, however, have a heavier 'Victorian' look about them. Projecting doorcases became fashionable. These carry rectangular fanlights, set beneath flat hooded canopies, supported on decorative consoles. Ten different fanlight types can be identified from this phase. In Railway Road and Portland Street the ground floor facades of some of the properties are stuccoed and scribed to imitate stonework in a rusticated fashion and some upper floor windows are provided with decorative moulded hoods.

In all phases the front gardens of the more expensive houses were enclosed with decorative cast iron railings, some of which survive. [53]

In general terms the quality of the architecture of this era of expansion is best described as a poorer provincial interpretation of that which prevailed in the capital. Builders would have been responsible for much of their own design work although White's Directory of 1854 lists three Lynn entries for architects; Cruso & Maberley, who designed the Corn Exchange and the Athenaeum and, as has been noted, were involved with Robert Mott on Lower Canada (in a surveying capacity), William Newham, the disgraced Chamberlain, who built properties on London Road, and his son, also called William.

There are, however, exceptions to this generalisation for a number of these buildings have been considered worthy of listed building status. In all there are 20 entries in the grade II category, comprising some 71 individual houses. These are to be found in London Road, Valinger's Road, Guanock Place, Portland Street, St. John's Terrace and Goodwin's Road.

99. 18 Blackfriars Road, built 1850. Elaborate Phase III style.

THE EXPANSION AREAS

The book's first tour guided the reader around the town's streets, as they existed in 1804, explaining the changes that had taken place between 1800 and 1870. The same approach has been adopted to describe the expansion areas, but instead of following a route on the ground the sequence for this second tour is arranged by the date that building first took place on each area. Newham's 1809 Plan has been used as a base to show the route.

The title given to each of the 17 areas is that commonly used before development occurred, but as many of the names will be new to the reader a more readily recognisable alterative is given in brackets. Each section contains a plan showing the nature and extent of development shortly after it was completed.

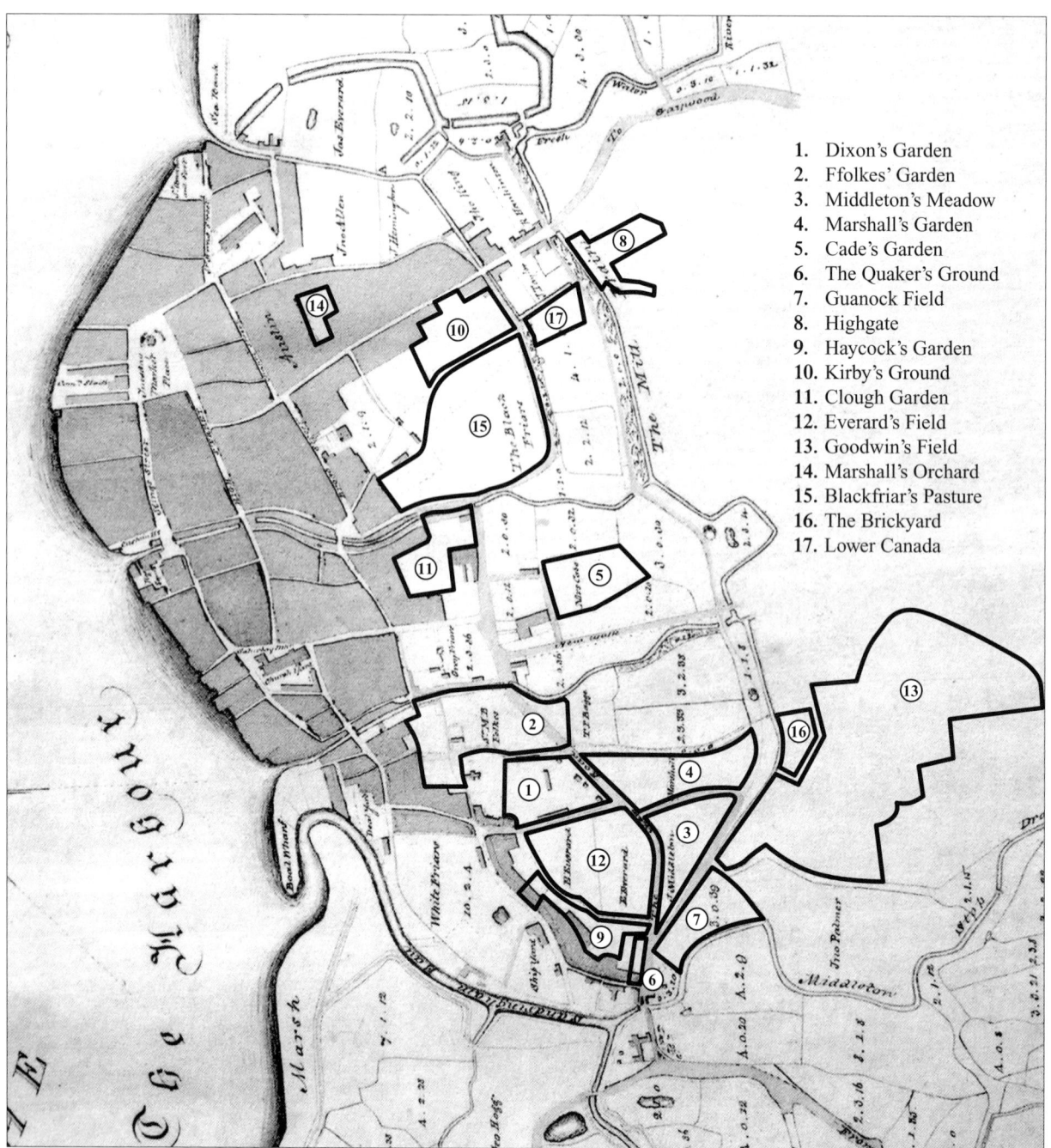

1. Dixon's Garden
2. Ffolkes' Garden
3. Middleton's Meadow
4. Marshall's Garden
5. Cade's Garden
6. The Quaker's Ground
7. Guanock Field
8. Highgate
9. Haycock's Garden
10. Kirby's Ground
11. Clough Garden
12. Everard's Field
13. Goodwin's Field
14. Marshall's Orchard
15. Blackfriar's Pasture
16. The Brickyard
17. Lower Canada

100. The Expansion Areas.

The commentaries start with a description of what the land was used for prior to development and this is followed by any mention made by contemporary writers. The most significant of these was William Armes who, in 1858, presented a series of papers to the Lynn Converzazione Society under the title, Memories of Lynn. [54]

As far as the actual housing development itself is concerned, information is given on the original landowner and the developer, together with any known builder. The development history of all the new streets is explained and where not obvious the meaning of each street name is given. In conclusion the subsequent fate of the individual housing areas is described.

Dixon's Garden (North of Valinger's Road) (1)

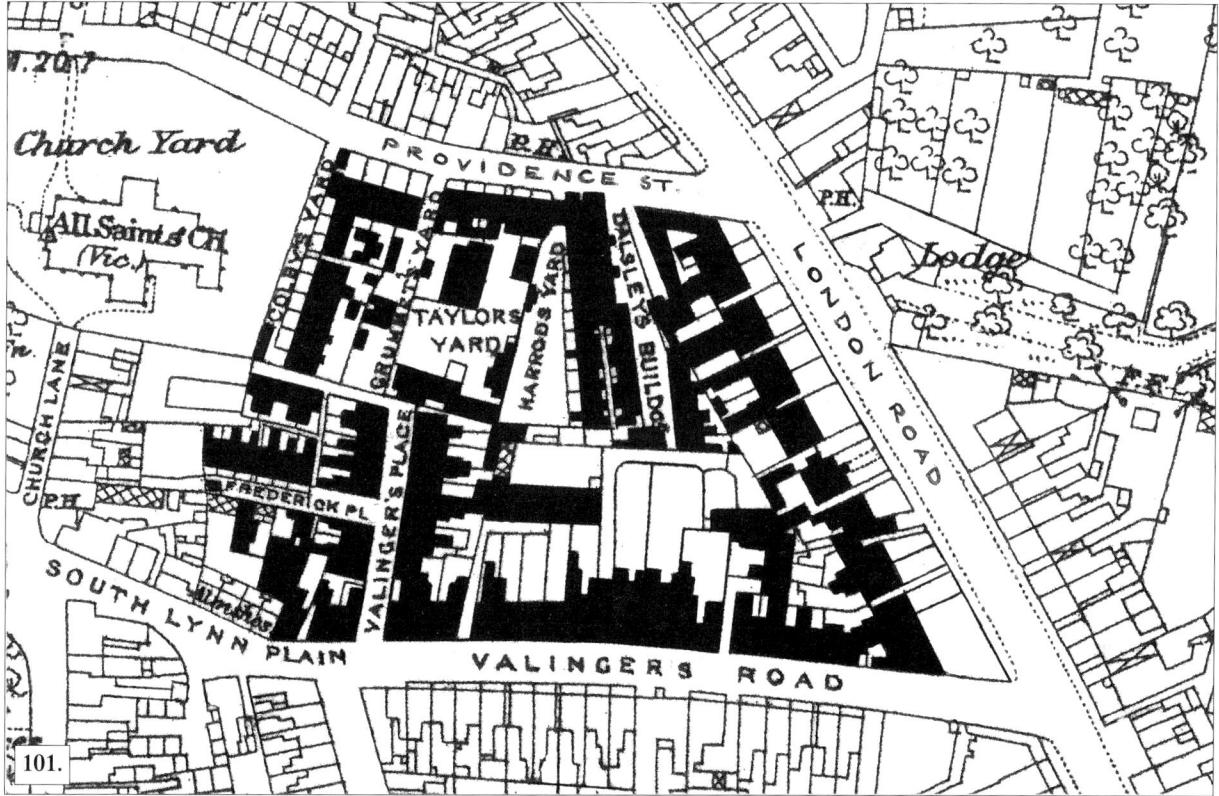

Robert Dixon owned this garden until his death in 1801. Under the provisions of his will his devisee, William Smith, was required to arrange for its disposal and distribute the proceeds amongst named beneficiaries. Shortly afterwards the construction of London Road provided a road frontage and Smith took the opportunity to market the land for development. Newham's 1806 Plan captures the moment with the description 'Late Garden ground now Building Land'.

His 1809 Plan shows buildings fronting the New Road and what was to become Providence Street and Valinger's Road. One of these bears the date 1807 and on the New Road frontage Thomas Begley built another, which that same year he sold to John Sugars.

These early houses are easily identifiable, as they are distinct from those that followed. Their emphasis is horizontal rather than vertical, they are detached or semi- detached, and their roofs are covered in red or black pantiles as Welsh slate was yet to be readily available in the town.

Smith also sold the backland and the 1809 Plan shows a long building in this location. This was a terrace of houses in Harrod's Yard, a corruption of the name of the man who built them, William Harwood. In 1806 he had bought a sizeable triangular section of the backland but sold half of it to Charles Wright. This became the site of Dalsley's Yard. Further west Smith sold land to Thomas

102. 100-102 London Road.

Gromitt on which was built Grummett's Yard, Taylor's Yard and Colby's Yard.

The remainder of the garden, the south-west portion, was sold in 1806 to Thomas King but, before he could develop it, he died and in 1808 his widow sold a small frontage piece to builder Matthew Doncaster for the construction of a single dwelling. Otherwise this part of the Garden remained largely undeveloped until August 1843 when John Sugars and John Smetham bought it and laid out Valinger's Place (named as such by the Paving Commissioners in 1849) and Frederick Place. The builders who developed plots there included James Brown, John Hall and Robert Wanford.

The fortunes of this area since then have been mixed. All the houses on the Providence Street frontage and the associated yards have been demolished, together with Valinger's Place and Frederick Place. The properties fronting London Road and Valinger's Road, however, have survived largely intact.

103. 105 London Road, built by Thomas Begley, c1806. Probably the first house to be built on London Road.

104. North Side of Valinger's Road showing a mixture of housing built between 1807 and 1850.

105. Harrod's Yard, built by William Harwood, c 1806.

Ffolkes' Garden (Hillington Square etc) (2)

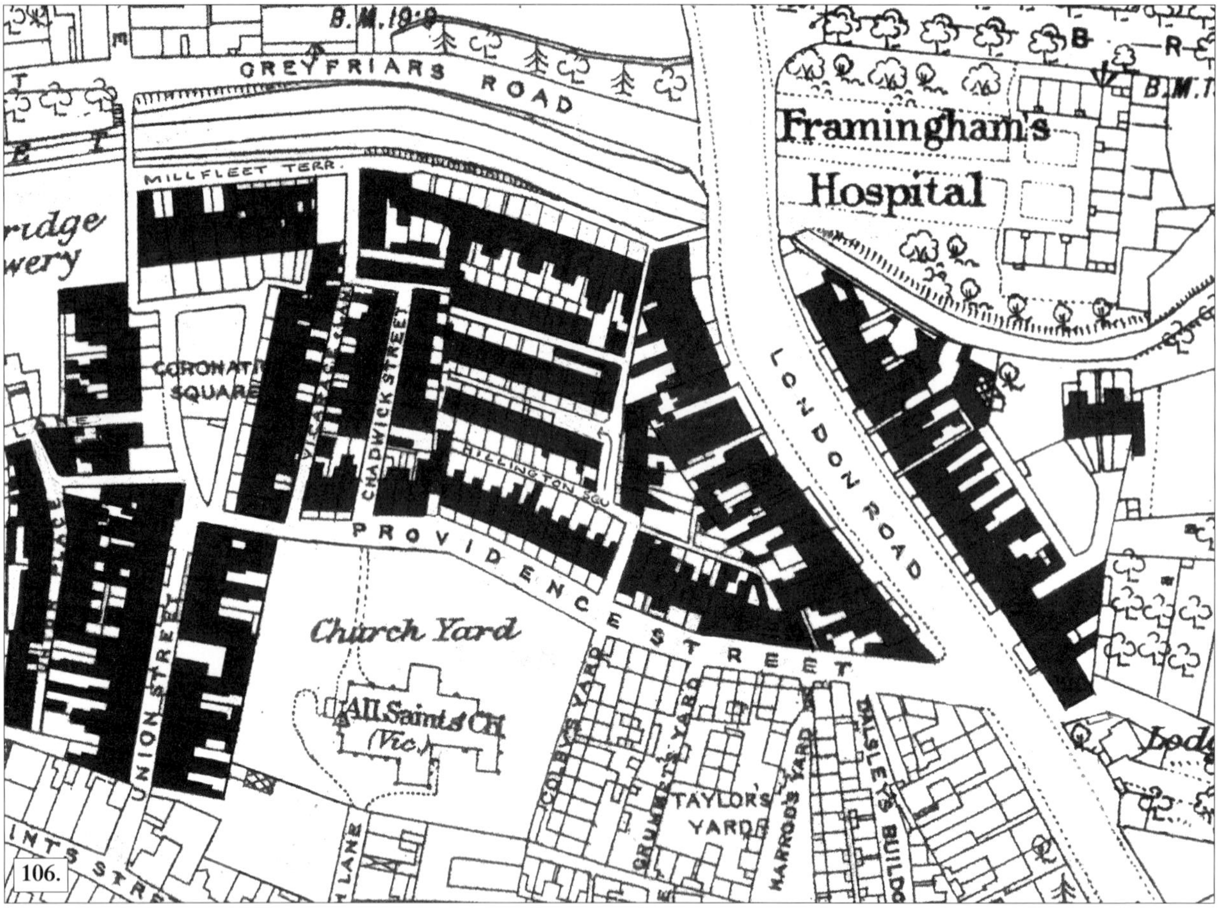

106.

This area comprised four sites, the largest of which was a piece of garden ground owned by the Ffolkes family of Hillington Hall. In 1858 William Armes described two of these sites in the following terms; 'From the fleet to All Saints' street are now what are called (satirically I suppose) Coronation square and Union street. In my boyhood none of these were there. Immediately opposite where we stand, and over the bridge, ran a high wall beside the fleet, being the north boundary of the site of Coronation square, which was then pasture land… The site of Union street was the garden of the father of Mr. Joseph Wales, whose descendants built over the space when building was a better speculation than it has since been'. [55]

A pasture west of the Jewish Cemetery was the first to be

107. East side of London Road, built between 1823 and 1829.

108. 1 London Road, built in 1841 on a site leased from the Corporation.

developed. The land was owned by Elizabeth Bell, widow of Henry Bell of Wallington Hall. In September 1821 it was sold to South Lynn builder, John Abraham, for £600. Shortly afterwards he built three terraces around a triangular shaped central garden space. This development he named Coronation Square after the recent crowning ceremony of George IV. Progress was such that in 1822 he was able to apply to the Paving Commissioners for street lamps. By 1835 there were 27 properties in Coronation Square, each yielding an average annual rent of £12 1s 2d.

In 1803 the New Road split the garden ground owned by Sir Martin Browne Ffolkes into two unequal parts, but he took no advantage of the house building opportunity this presented. On his death in 1821, however, his son and heir, Sir William Browne Ffolkes, immediately set about marketing it for development. Unlike most of the other landowners he retained the freehold, seemingly selling on a 99-year lease to merchant and miller, William Ayre, who, acting as overall developer, sold plots for building.

In common with the rest of London Road, the frontage strips were treated separately for development purposes and between 1823 and 1829 irregular terraces were formed on both sides of the road by a variety of owners including builder John Sugars, the elder. Being only two storeys high, these houses did not have the same architectural impact as many of those further south. On the western side the development included a Primitive Methodist Chapel, built in 1824, and on the east, James Wright's St. James' School.

On both sides of London Road, against the Millfleet, lay plots that were outside the area of this development, as they were owned by the Corporation. However, in 1836, the plot on the eastern side was leased to Joseph Fyson, who proceeded to build the elegant house that is now No 1, and in 1841 the plot on the western side was leased to Thomas Halifax, who built what is now No 129.

Development of the backland started around 1823, producing Hillington Square, Millfleet Terrace and the northern frontage of Providence Street. William Ayre maintained a major interest in this development. In September 1829 an application by him 'and other persons interested in certain buildings lately erected next Mill Fleet and now called Millfleet Terrace for permission to have a right of way across the Corporation Ground adjoining the new bridge on the London Road' was turned down. By 1835 Hillington Square contained

109. Union Street looking south, c1965.

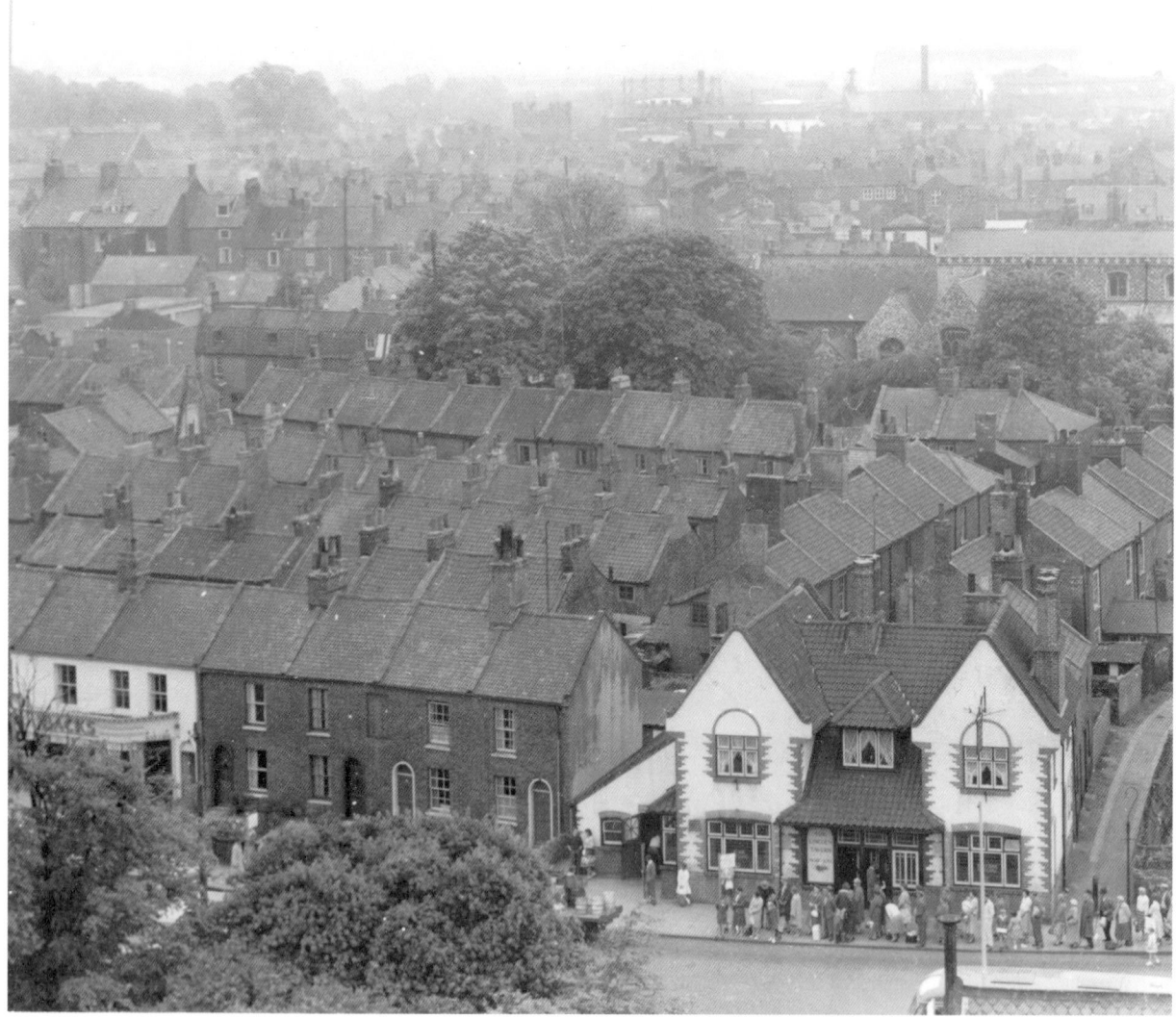

110. Bird's eye view of Ffolkes' Garden, looking south, c1960. It shows the whole area from Hillington Square on the left to Coronation Square on the right.

25 houses with an average annual rental of £10 10s.

The next piece of land in this area to be developed was that described by Armes as belonging to the father of Mr. Joseph Wales. In May 1831 it was reported to the Paving Commissioners that a new street to connect Coronation Square with All Saints Street was under consideration. By then the land was owned by Robert and Henry Cook and their wives. The new street was called Union Street and by December 1836 John Laird, Richard Hall, and other builders had made sufficient progress with their work to enable the Paving Commissioners to assume responsibility for street maintenance.

The final piece of land to be developed here was the site of the South Lynn Vicarage. On 7th September 1850 the Advertiser gave notice of an auction of,' All that piece of BUILDING GROUND, situate in the Parish of South Lynn, near Coronation Square, as formerly occupied by the Vicars of the said Parish…'(South Lynn). The old vicarage had been demolished and Lynn attorney John Nurse Chadwick bought the site. In November 1850 he asked the Paving Commissioners to construct a drain in Vicarage Lane to connect to one he proposed to construct on his site. This they agreed to do. The site was just wide enough for a single street of houses, which its developer named Chadwick Street after himself. [56]

With the exception of the properties fronting London Road, the housing on all four sites was demolished in the late 1960s to make way for the present day Hillington Square.

111. The west side of London Road, built between 1823 and 1829.

Middleton's Meadow (Windsor Row etc)(3)

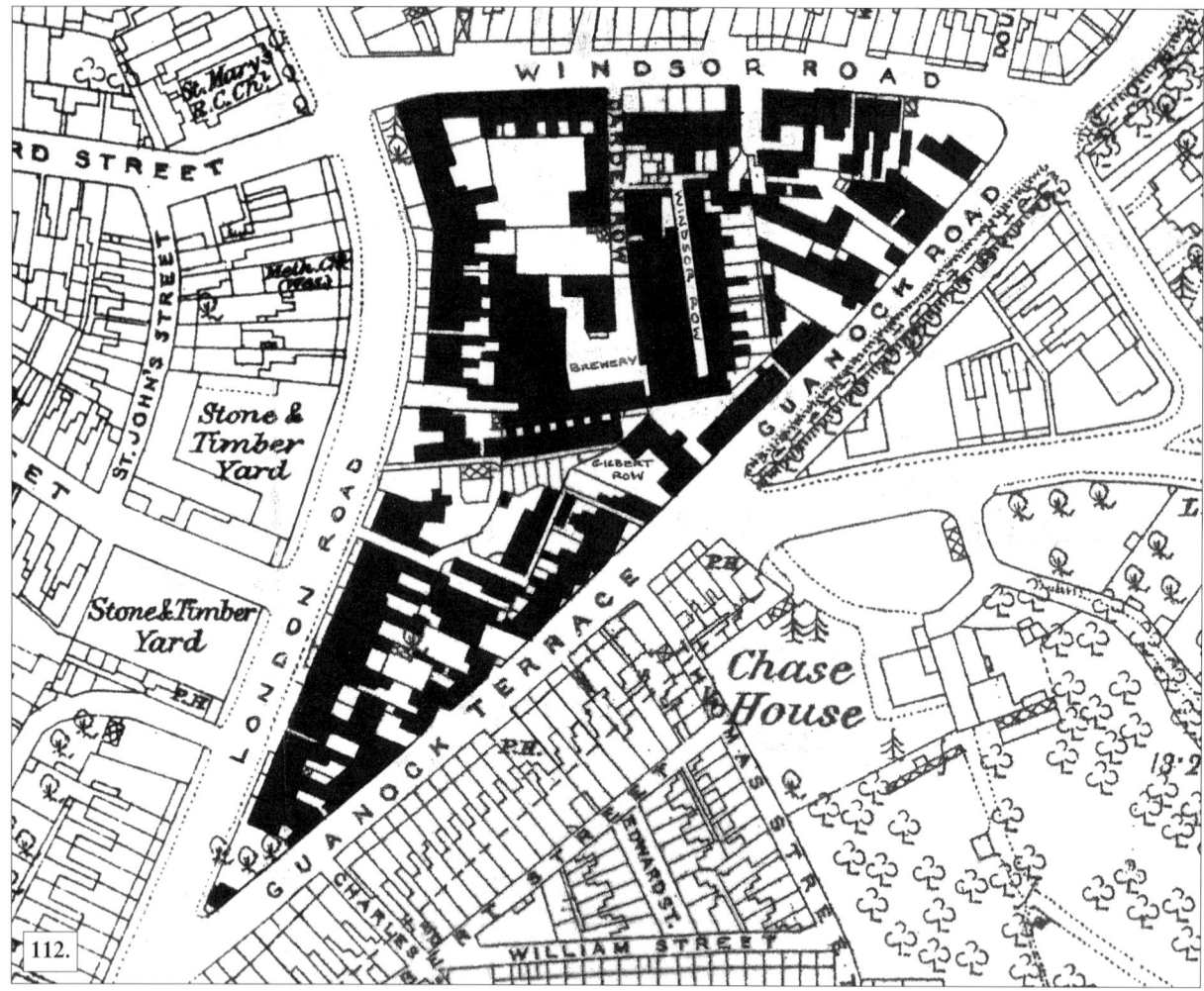

On Newham's 1806 Plan this triangular shaped piece of land comprised a two-acre meadow in the ownership of John Middleton, and a pasture known as the Shoulder of Mutton Piece.

Armes commented that; 'On the *opposite side* of the London road, (from Checker Street) where now stands Mrs. Burcham's and other houses, all was meadow land, and, strange as it must now appear, upon that spot, year after year, have I seen exhibitions of rustic sports, such as climbing greased poles, jumping in sacks, catching (or failing to catch) pigs with tallowed tails; and I do now often meet a most respectable inhabitant whom I remember as a boy being successful upon that spot in a race for a hat'. [57]

Like most owners Middleton did not seek to exploit his frontage to the New Road and it was not until the early 1820s that development of this site commenced. On 11th March 1822 the Paving Commissioners considered a request from William Newham, now working as an architect/builder, to make a barrel drain on the east side of London Road, in front of a piece of land he had purchased for building. Prior to this, in November 1820, Susan Goulden had bought a plot on this frontage and subsequently had a house built and in October 1822 builder Edward Mitchley sold John Armes a pair of houses there. The properties completing this frontage at the northern end were not built until the 1840s.

The southern frontage of Windsor Road was also built in the 1820s as were the buildings fronting Guanock Terrace. By the time Wood's 1830 Plan was published the outer perimeter of the meadow had been developed. The only buildings on the backland, however, were a terrace of seven houses called Gilbert Row after their owner, stonemason William Gilbert and the start of Garden Row.

113. The east side of London Road, built in the early 1820s by, amongst others, William Newham.

In 1833 Richard Checker bought a piece of backland from Benjamin Garner and developed Windsor Row. Checker laid out the road for builders, including John Southwell, James Watering and Thomas Whitby.

Also in 1833, William Benn, by virtue of an authority given to him in 1817, following the bankruptcy of John Middleton, sold to shipbuilder, William Richardson, a substantial part of the two-acre meadow, on which he built a terrace of houses as an extension to Garden Row.

In 1858 Richardson's widow, Sarah, sold most of these houses to Mary Ann Boothby of Downham Market. These were later demolished to make way for the London Road Brewery, which in the latter part of the 19th Century was owned by John Jex Rolfe.

Today the frontage buildings on London Road and Windsor Road are largely intact, but several of those on Guanock Terrace and all the buildings erected in the backland have been demolished. Their site is now occupied by Old Brewery Court (a sheltered housing scheme) and a public car park.

114. Garden Row looking south, c1934.

115. The east side of London Road.

116. Gilbert's Row off London Road, c1934.

117. The north side of Windsor Road.

118. The north side of Guanock Terrace showing workshops and warehouses backing onto London Road.

Marshall's Garden (North of Windsor Road) (4)

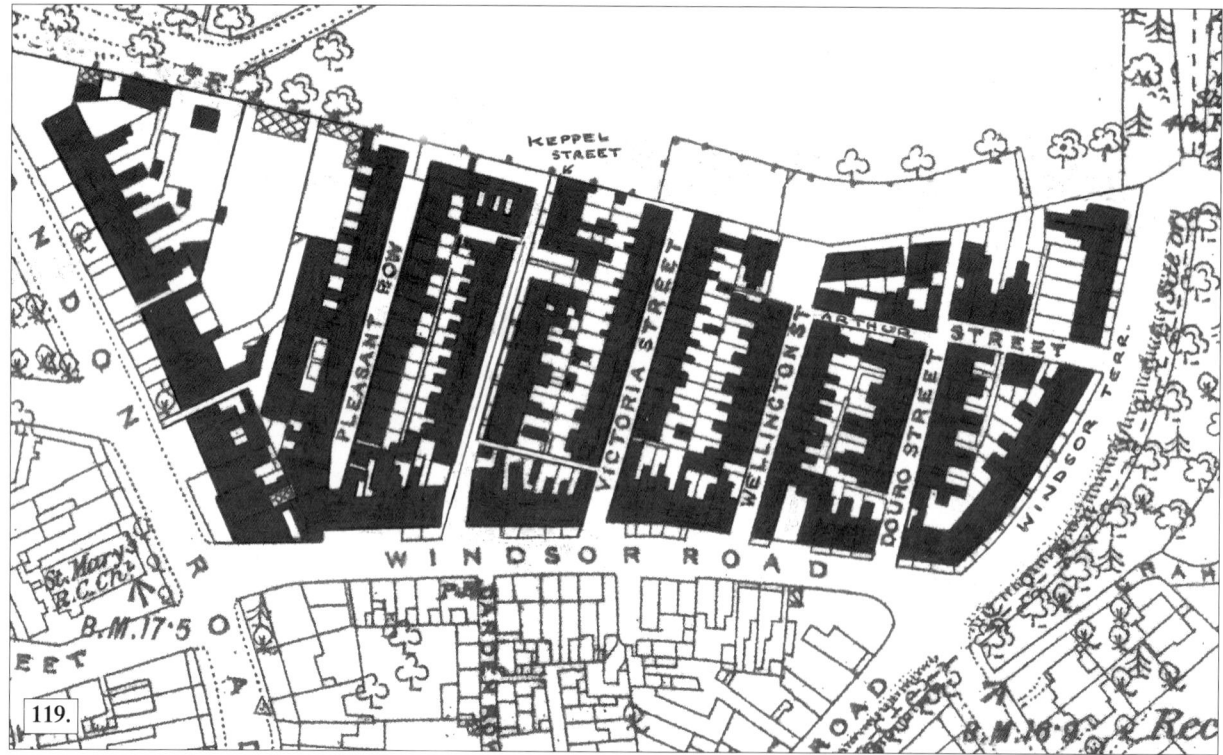

This area was one of Thomas Marshall's many market gardens and it is shown as such on Newham's Plans of 1806 and 1809. The frontage it gained to the New Road in 1804 was not developed until the early 1820s. By 1830 the first piece of development land with access onto Windsor Place (later Road) had been sold and developed as Pleasant Row. The name of this street was seemingly a misnomer for in 1835 the annual rent of its 21 houses averaged at no more that £3 4s 6¼d, the lowest then existing in the town, even lower than the lowest rents in the yards.

Disposing of his land in an easterly direction, Marshall sold the next strip to carpenter William Triance in March 1834. On this Triance built Keppel Street, named after Major George Keppel, a Lynn parliamentary candidate. He also built Victoria Street on the land beyond that, naming it after the newly crowned Queen. He was selling houses there by October 1837.

As the development progressed so the northern frontage of Windsor Place kept pace with it. By 1841 the eastern boundary of the development ran along the back of Victoria Street.

The remainder of the Garden was developed in the late 1840s/early 1850s. On 3rd November 1852 the Paving Commissioners confirmed that the new streets in this area should be called Wellington Street, Douro Street and Arthur Street, all commemorating the Duke of Wellington, who had recently died. They also decided that Windsor Place should become Windsor Road. At the following meeting the Commissioners considered a request from the owners and occupiers of the area to rename Wellington Street, Pashley Street, a request they turned down. If this had been accepted, it would have given the street a third name for it had started life in 1850 as West Street.

Marshall died in 1849 and it was his devisees who sold the remaining land for the final phase. In 1850 William Candler bought part of the land that became Wellington Street, but sold it on to William Seapey, who seems to have been the street's main developer.

None of this housing exists today, as it was all demolished under slum clearance procedures in the late 1960s.

120. The east side of London Road, built in the 1820s.

121. Windsor Road, looking east, c1965.

122. The north side of Windsor Road, looking through an archway into Pleasant Row, c1965.

123. Keppel Street, looking north, c1965.

124. Wellington Street, west side, looking north, c1965.

125. Douro Street, east side, looking north, c1965.

Cade's Garden (Wood Street/South Street) (5)

Cade's Garden took its name from Mary Cade who occupied it, then owned it, in the late 18th/early 19th Centuries. In 1767 it was described as 'formly called the Brick Yard then converted into a Garden Ground'.[58] It was surrounded on three sides by Corporation owned land, which explains why the modern day housing, built on the site, seems to intrude into the Walks.

In 1812 it was bought by market gardener Thomas Woods for £900. In 1823 he sold it to John Palmer of South Lynn who intended to develop it for housing. Laying out two inter-connecting streets he began marketing frontage plots to builders and other investors. Rather unimaginatively he called his streets South Street and North Street. The builders who purchased land from him included George Adcock, William Bailey, John Murrell, William Salmon Rolin, Edward Walker and Thomas Whitby.

By 1830 the whole of South Street had houses on both sides, but North Street remained largely undeveloped until the mid-1840s when the Paving Commissioners renamed it Wood Street to avoid confusion with the other North Streets which existed in the town. This renaming took place on 10th June 1847.

The area suffered bomb damage in World War II and, after the war, the Corporation built houses and bungalows on the affected sites. In the late 1970s the remainder of the older housing was demolished, to be replaced eventually by the houses that stand there today.

127. Wood Street, south side, looking east, c1965.

128. South Street, north side, looking east, c1965.

The Quaker's Ground (Buckingham Terrace) (6)

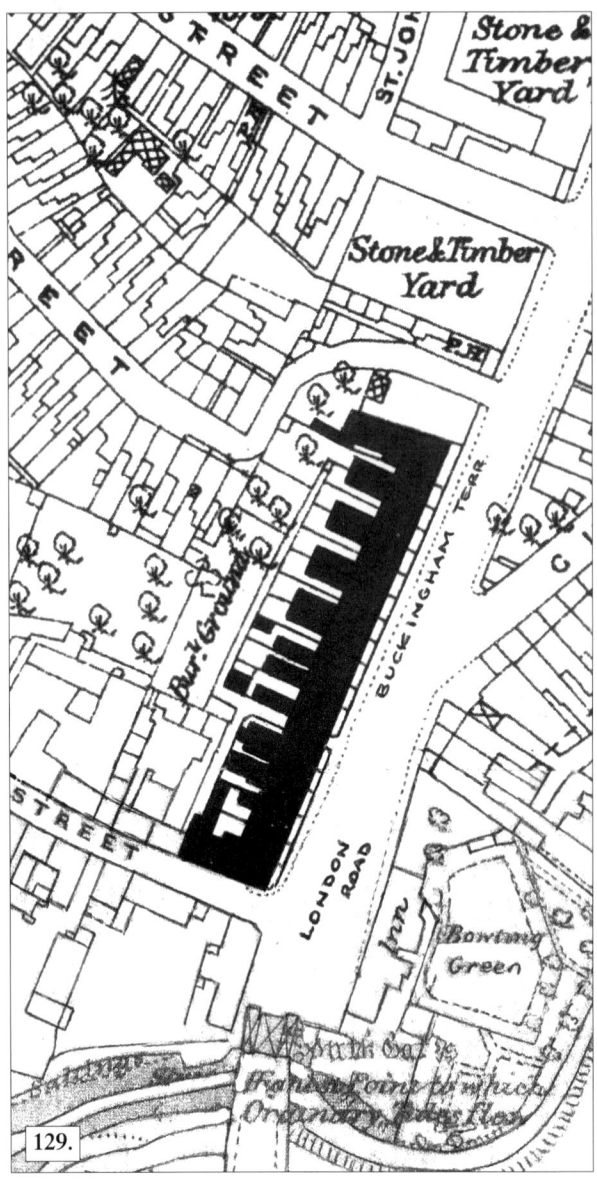

129.

Long before the construction of London Road, the Quakers owned land and cottages in South Lynn that had been bequeathed to them by Thomas Buckingham, a late 17th Century Lynn merchant. The cottages fronted the northern side of Southgate Street, at its eastern end. Behind them lay a pasture that in 1804 gained a frontage to the New Road. [59]

Newham's 1806 Plan describes this pasture as 'land for building', but it was not until 1821 that the first steps were taken to achieve this aim. On 20th August that year the Quakers applied to the Paving Commissioners for a small piece of land to level their frontage as they intended to let the site on building leases. A year later their minutes record that an application had been made for the land, and in June 1824 it was observed that 'the cottages in South Lynn are in a very delapidated condition'. [60] In September it was noted that 'a person … has made inquiry respecting this estate apparently with a desire to have the premises on a building lease' and on 20th June 1825 it was decided to pull down the cottages and let the site, in conjunction with the adjoining pasture. As a result James Gathergood was granted a 99-year lease from 25th March 1825, for £45 per annum, excluding the roadway at the northern end, which was let to Giles Haycock to access his field.

Gathergood was a builder and he quickly set about constructing a terrace of houses, but on 10th October 1826 he died leaving his widow, Maria, to complete the work. As part of the transaction with the Quakers, Gathergood had been allowed a 50% remission on the rent for two years. Shortly after he died his widow applied for this remission to be extended for a further two years 'in consequence of the death of her husband causing great delay in the erection of the buildings….' In the event this was unnecessary for, at the expiration of the first two years (25th March 1827), she sold the lease to

130. The partly built Buckingham Terrace as seen through the South Gate in 1827. Engraving by William Oldmeadow.

Edmund Trundle of Swaffham.

Trundle continued building the terrace, but he too applied for a remission in the rent 'as I have not been so fortunate as to succeed in the enterprise'. His letter of 17th June 1829 contains much useful detail, especially in relation to the requirements of the lease. He stated that all the buildings had been finished in the first year i.e. before 25th March 1828 and that 'the Writings express, that a sum not less than Three Thousand Pounds should be expended thereon, whereas I have expended nearly Five Thousand Pounds, by Wch means your estate is benefitted, being more durable, by making the kitchens & back offices better & larger than the specification; by making boundry walls to each house seperately; by making the front fencing; instead of wood pales on four inch brickwork, on nine inch brickwork with stone Coping & Iron Pallisades wch will doubtless at the end of the lease be nearly as good as at present; in other respects also the Buildings are done in the most substantial & workmanlike manner, that I think I may be allowed to say would not have been the Case had they gone on as at first by selling every allotment; there might in that case have been as many purchasers as there are houses; & it is not probable the Buildings would have been done in that uniform & substantial manner they now are'. In conclusion he lamented that he had built 14 houses but, only eight of them had been let.

In 1830 the strip leased to Haycock was transferred to Trundle as Haycock had sold his land for the construction of Checker Street. This then

131. Buckingham Terrace. Typical house fronts. Note the fanlights and the plat band.

became part of the garden of the northern most house in Buckingham Terrace, the name given to the whole development, to commemorate the man who had originally given the land to the Quakers.

Gathergood built the first four houses (Nos 60-63 London Road) and Trundle the remaining 14 (Nos 64-77 London Road). Between them they were responsible for creating the longest uniform Georgian terrace in the town. [61]

132. Buckingham Terrace, looking north.

Guanock Field (Guanock Terrace etc) (7)

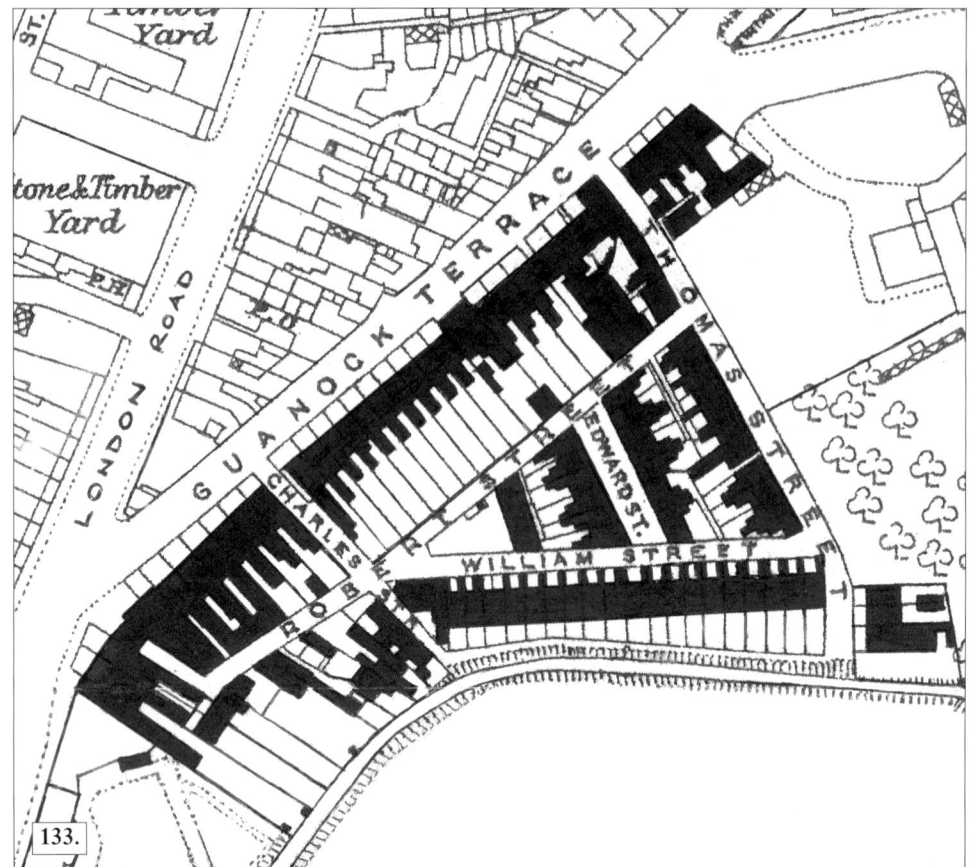

By 1830 the fine three storeyed terrace, called Guanock Place, had been completed, together with the more modest Guanock Terrace and the terrace that fronted the Middleton Stop Drain. This was known as Begley's Row suggesting that it was built or owned by the Begley family of builders. In 1864 it was renamed Esk Terrace and the road behind it was called William Street at the same time.

The backland between Guanock Terrace and Begley's

The Guanock Field was part of the Corporation Estate and prior to its development was let to Alderman Thomas Allen. On 29th September 1825 the Corporation agreed to sell the field to attorney Charles Goodwin for £1,200 in order to raise money to rebuild the Grammar School House in St. James' Street. In January 1826 Goodwin did further business with the Corporation, arranging a land exchange where the field adjoined the Crown Inn, in order to improve the shape of his site.

In selling the land the Corporation stipulated that Goodwin was not to build nearer to the Terrace Walk than the foot of the bank, or the perpendicular line of the water on the west side of the ditch adjoining the Walk. He had also to make a barrel drain from the south-west corner of the boundary of the land to discharge into the fleet near the South Gate.

134. Guanock Terrace, built by Charles Goodwin in the late 1820s.

135. Guanock Place, a good quality terrace built by Charles Goodwin in the late 1820s.

Row remained vacant for some years after the completion of the initial development, but towards the end of the 1840s Thomas Street was built to complete the triangle, being named as such by the Paving Commissioners in 1850. Much later in the 19th century Edward Street was built on the remaining section of the backland. All the development on the Guanock Field remains intact.

136. Begley's Row, now William Street.

Highgate (Front Row etc) (8)

The area of land on which Highgate was built lay in the parish of Gaywood, just to the south-east of the old mediaeval East Gate. Being outside the control of the authorities in Lynn and some distance from the village of Gaywood it acquired the characteristics and facilities of a separate community.

The name Highgate probably derives from the area's close proximity to the East Gate, perhaps having a similar origin to the place of the same name in London which is thought to be a shortened version of 'high toll gate'. [62]

In 1810 when the Gaywood Enclosure Map was produced only one house existed on this land, owned by Lynn surgeon Barnard Middleton. It stood by a track which led south from the Gaywood Road, between land owned by Middleton on the east and that of Sir Martin Ffolkes on the west. [63] On Middleton's death in 1817 the land passed to his widow Elizabeth and when in 1824 she died it seems to have been acquired by seedsman Charles Adams, who may already have been its tenant.

Development probably started the following year under the guiding hand of Adams and by 1831 a sizeable settlement had been established. The Gaywood Tithe Map of 1839 gives a clear picture of this fledgling community. [64] In total 74 properties lined the west side of Front Row and both sides of Double Row. Charles Adams owned 12 of them and builder Edward Broadway a further 8.

In the 1840s Garden Row was added, with links through to Front Row and Double Row taking its name from the fact that it was built on market garden land owned by Adams.

138. Double Row, looking east, c1955.

On 24th April 1847 the Advertiser reported that; 'We cannot here omit to notice the filling up of a large ditch along Highgate, ... thus turning a stagnant and unhealthy pool, into a pleasant and healthy spot, increasing the value of the property adjacent full fifty per cent'. This ditch ran along the western side of Front Row and seems to have been deterring the development of the land lying between it and the Gaywood River. This now changed and by 1849 house building was in progress. As the site widened towards the South so frontage development gave way to Stag Row and Exhibition Terrace, a name that places the latter shortly after the Great Exhibition of 1851.

Today little remains of old Highgate except for the Primitive Methodist Chapel and a house alongside. The remainder was subject to slum clearance in the 1960s, making way for local authority housing.

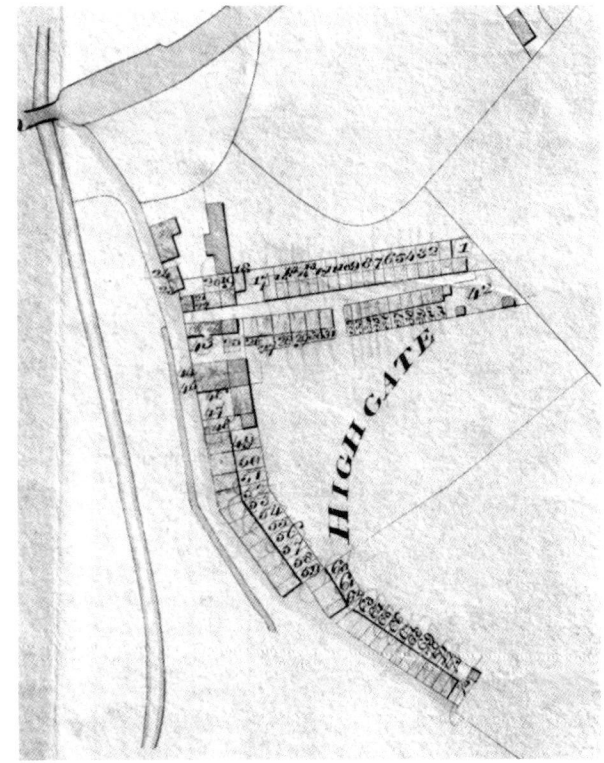

139. Plan of Highgate in 1839. Extract from the Gaywood Tithe Map.

140. Garden Row, looking east, c1955.

141. Front Row, looking south, c1955.

Haycock's Garden (Checker Street) (9)

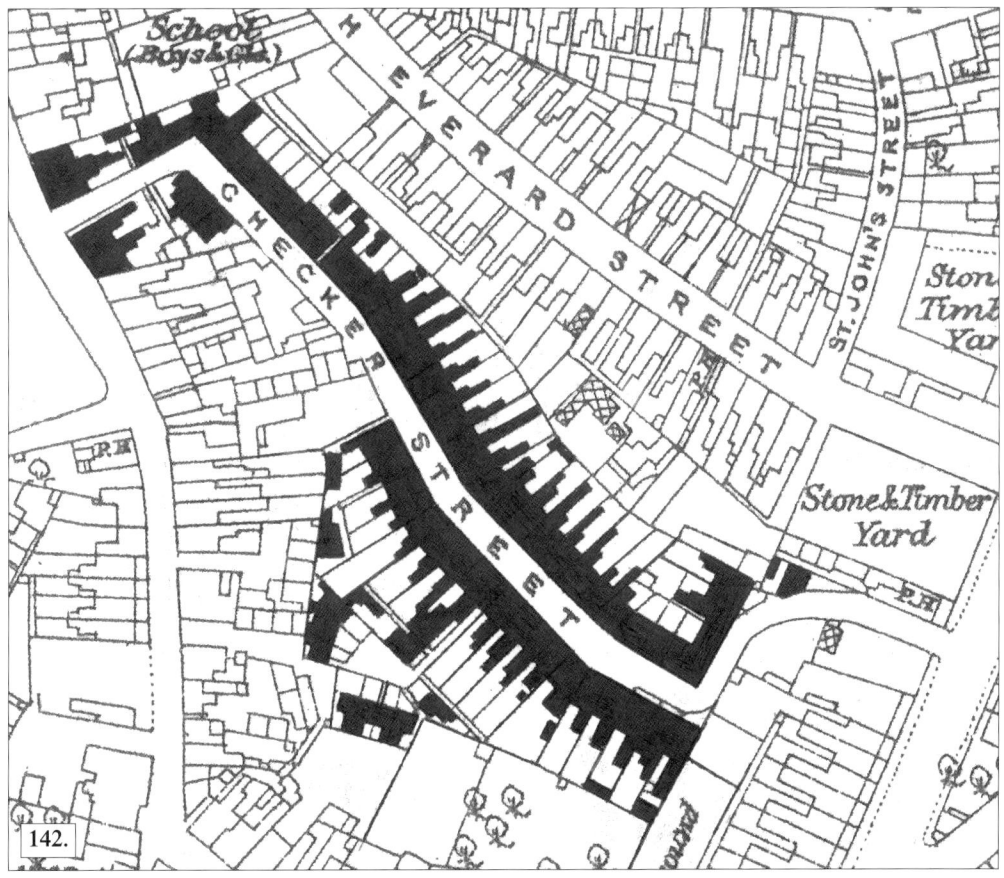

142.

Prior to development this site was a market garden owned by maltster Giles Haycock and leased to Thomas Britton, a butcher living in Friar Street. [65]

Armes described it in the following terms; '...where now runs New Checker street, was a large market garden, stretching from the London road to the old South Lynn workhouse, and from the south line of Everard's field... to the wall of the back gardens of the houses in Friar's street. When that garden was built upon it was a sad loss to Friar's street. Having spent my boyhood in that spot I can testify strongly to this fact. Until then all was open behind Friars' street to the north. The houses had all pleasant and considerable gardens, behind the walls of which stretched the kitchen garden and orchard, and beyond the open space of Everard's field. Many a time in the early summer's morning have I, in one of those gardens, listened with delight to the many songs of the little birds as they hopped about and above me, while the swallows in vast numbers would be spread in warm sun upon the roofs of the houses, pecking out the mortar with their long bills. On such mornings, the housewives of Friars' street were wont to take their baskets to the garden wall, and bargain for the potatoes, carrots, cabbages, etc which were then cut or dug for the oc-

143. Checker Street, south side looking west.

144. 8 Checker Street. House built in 1834 by Richard Checker for his own occupation

casion. But, on a fatal day, a millionaire and a lawyer looked wistfully upon the spot. They held sundry consultations, all, of course (as such consultations usually are), for the benefit of the public; and, at length, the fences were broken down, the ground was planned for the New Checker street, and contractors' carts of bricks and lime soon cut up and obliterated the kitchen garden'. [66]

The two developers referred to were Richard Checker and local attorney/banker Lewis Weston Jarvis. In 1830 they bought the land in equal shares from Haycock for £800 and laid out a street 16 feet wide, linking London Road to Friar Street. This they called Checker Street after Richard, but the word 'New' was soon added to avoid confusion with Chequer Street, which, despite being renamed King Street in 1809, was still being referred to by its former name at this time.

With the street set out, the developers began selling plots to investors and builders in the usual way. Wood's 1830 Plan shows that building started at the north-eastern corner with a property, which, later became the Bowling Green public house. By 1835 the whole street had been developed and the average annual rental for the 52 houses was £7 3s 4½d.

As early as 1832 the developers applied to the Paving Commissioners for street lamps but the response was not positive. In 1835 the occupiers asked for a paved channel to take the water off the street, as it was in a very bad state, but this too was refused. The developers themselves made the same request in 1836, but were also turned down. However, when in 1839 it was reported to the Paving Commissioners 'that Checker Street is in very bad repair for want of a few Loades of Gravel in the worst places', action was taken, with the surveyor being ordered to procure five or six loads of fine gravel to keep the street in good order for the year.

The street was originally laid out with front gardens or spaces belonging to the house owners and no footways, but in 1845 the Paving Commissioners decided to lay footways 'in all cases where the Owners of the adjoining Houses consent to give up the frontages or small spaces between their houses and the Street but that no drain be made there until all the Owners have give up their Frontages'. The take up seems to have been poor for a similar resolution was passed in 1855, but eventually two footways were laid out. How different the street would look today if this measure had not been implemented. This street of neat terrace cottages remains largely as is was built.

145. Checker Street looking north.

Kirby's Ground (Kirby Street etc) (10)

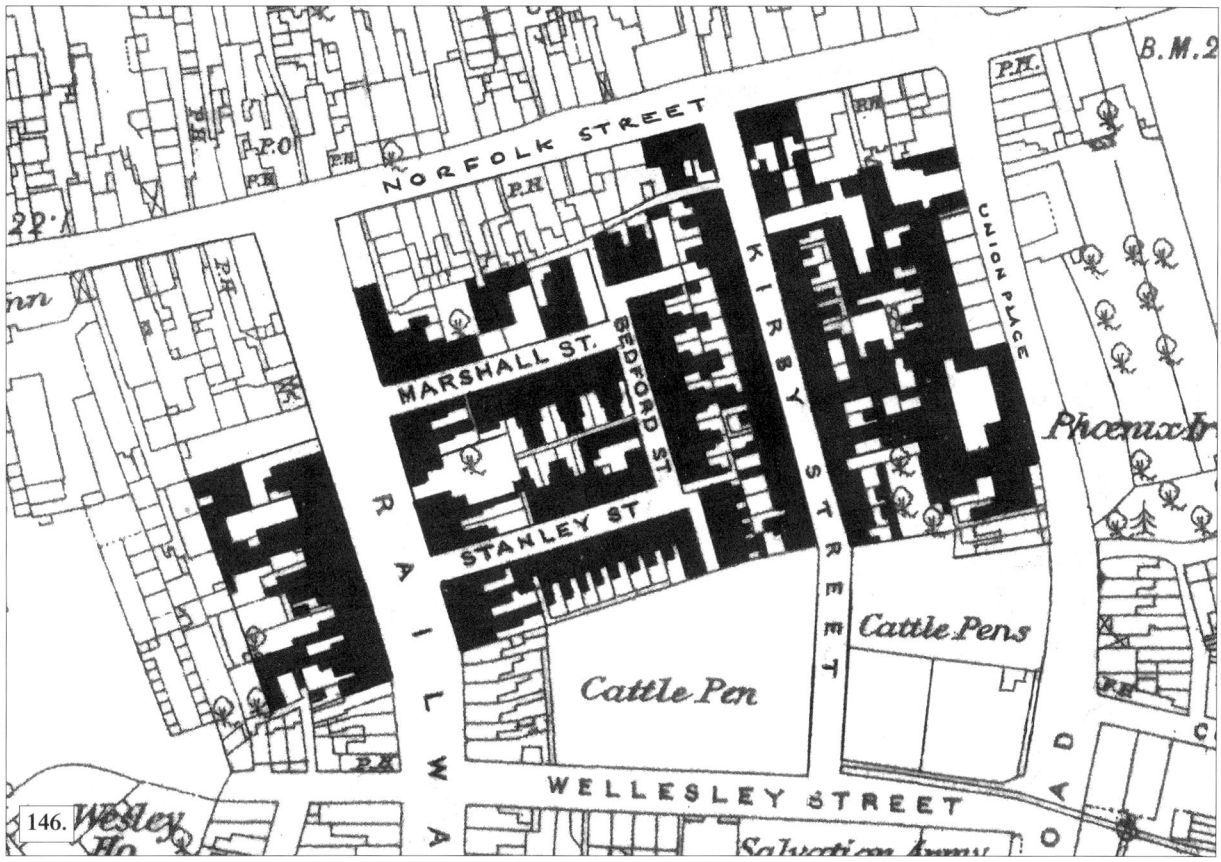

146.

Kirby's Ground took its name from the family who once owned it. On Newham's 1806 Plan it is described as garden ground and at that time it had an open aspect to the Echo Road and a substantial frontage to Norfolk Street.

Wood's 1830 Plan describes this market garden as belonging to Thomas Marshall. By then Union Place had been built on the Echo Road frontage and in Norfolk Street two blocks of three houses had been constructed, with a gap between them to access the backland. Isaac Dobson was responsible for at least the western block.

Soon after 1830 Marshall laid out what was to become Kirby Street and set about selling plots. Purchasers included Edward Broadway, who had recently been involved with the Highgate development.

By 12th September 1836 sufficient houses had been built to prompt a petition to the Paving Commissioners, to have the street 'paved lighted and cleansed'. The Commissioners, however, refused the request, as the street was not a thoroughfare. By 1841 the development of Kirby Street was virtually complete.

The remainder of Kirby's Ground lay undeveloped until after the death of Marshall in

147. 62-67 Norfolk Street, built c1830 as part of the Kirby Street development.

148. North end of Railway Road, c1910.

1849. In 1850 his devisees, Cornell Fison and William Armes, sold this land to William Laurence of Peterborough. He laid out three streets, which in December 1851 the Paving Commissioners named Marshall Street, Stanley Street (after one of the town's Members of Parliament), and Bedford Street (possibly commemorating local man Bedford Russell who lived in nearby Union Place). Builders William Aggar and James and William Purdy constructed houses in these streets.

Much of the area was subjected to clearance in the 1960s although the buildings fronting Railway Road and Norfolk Street survive, together with the southern side of Marshall Street.

149. South side of Marshall Street.

Clough Garden (South of South Clough Lane) (11)

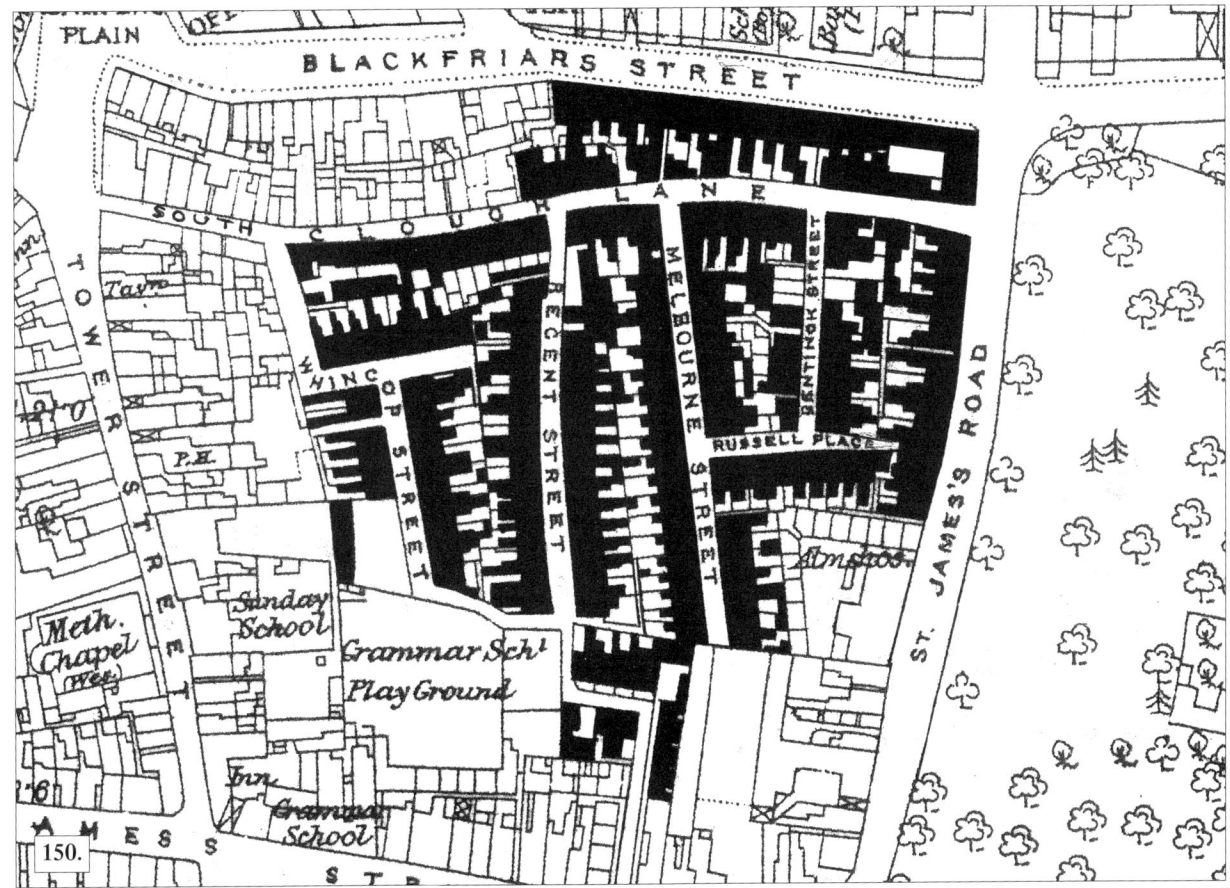

The Clough Garden was owned by the Whincop family most notably Robert, who was Town Clerk and the first clerk to the Paving Commissioners, and later his son, George Raynor.

Newham's 1806 Plan shows buildings fronting the south side of South Clough Lane, at both ends and in the middle, but otherwise the site was open. By 1830 the frontage to St. James' Road had been developed, probably by the Whin family.

The development opportunity created by William Candler out of the Purfleet was described earlier. Shortly after completing this work, his attention was drawn to an adjoining site, the Clough Garden. In January 1836, together with fellow builder John Southwell, he bought a large tract of this land from George Whincop for £955. On this would be built Bentinck Street, Russell Place (initially Cross Street) and Melbourne Street (all named after prominent politicians), but not by Candler and Southwell for, in November 1836, they sold the land, with the exception of what would become the western side of Melbourne Street, to Charles Goodwin for £635 6s 8d.

It was Goodwin who developed the site, selling off plots in the usual way. Progress was such that in March 1839 he bought the next section from Whincop for £487 and laid out Regent Street. The Poor Rate books chart the progress of this development with Melbourne Street being first mentioned in mid-1837, Bentinck Street and Russell Place in mid-1838, and Regent Street in the Spring of 1840. [67]

Whincop retained the rest of the garden as a buffer between the new housing and the rear of the properties in Tower Street, (which included his own family home, Whincop House), apart from the remaining frontage to South Clough Lane. This piece he sold in July 1840 to Goodwin's partner Frederick Partridge with the proviso that a wall was built on its southern and western boundaries. He also stipulated that no windows were to overlook his garden.

On Whincop's death in 1846, his devisees sold this remaining land to hatter, John Keed, who proceeded to develop Whincop Street and Whincop Place. In October 1849 these streets were taken over by the Paving Commissioners, marking the completion of the development of the Clough Garden.

All the houses except one (26 South Clough Lane) were demolished in the late 1960s as part of the town centre redevelopment proposals. Today the site is occupied by the town's swimming pool and a multi-storey car park.

151. Bentinck Street, west side, looking north, c1965.

152. Melbourne Street, looking south, c1965.

153. Russell Place, south side, looking west, c1965.

154. Whincop Street, west side, looking north, c1965.

Everard's Field (North Everard Street and South Everard Street etc) (12)

155.

Armes commented that prior to its development, 'all the space from Valinger's road to the north end of Buckingham terrace was an open field known as *Everard's Field*, and was fenced next the road by a wooden railing, and next the Valinger's road by one of the ordinary Lynn ditches'. [68]

In 1804, when the construction of the New Road gave this field a prominent eastern frontage, the then owner, Edward Everard, ignored the development opportunity this represented. In 1829 his son and namesake succeeded him and shortly thereafter he sold a plot of land at the junction of London Road and Valinger's Road to builder John Sugars, the younger, for £346 5s. Sugars, perhaps with the encouragement of Everard, seems to have set his sights on creating a prestigious frontage to London Road, being responsible for several of the more substantial houses, on the western side, including two on this plot.

Nothing more seems to have happened until March 1837 when Everard offered the Paving Commissioners 'part of the Frontage of his Field on the East Side of the London road at the same price at which he is selling the land for Building'. In the event the suggested improvement was thought to be too costly and the offer was rejected.

That same year Everard sold a site at the northern end of what was to be South Everard Street to baker, George Medlock, abutting a 'newly made road or street intended to be called South Street'. This seems to mark the start of the development of the housing area, which is now popularly known as The Everards.

Progress, however, seems to have been rather slow for it was not until 6th June 1842 that an application was made so that 'the Roads across the Pasture in South Lynn which Mr. Everard has sold

156. 96-97 London Road, built by John Sugars in 1830.

for Building may be permanently placed under the care and superintendence of the Commissioners'. The Commissioners' response is instructive in that they were prepared to take over the stretch of South Everard Street from Valinger's Road to the junction with North Everard Street because of it 'having been formed into a Street by Buildings on each Side'. They were not, however, prepared to assume responsibility for the remainder until January 1843.

Initially the two main streets were called North Street and South Street. Linking these was John Street, which on 15th August 1842 was renamed St. John's Street. On 17th November 1847 North Street and South Street were renamed North Everard Street and South Everard Street respectively, to remove the confusion that existed because there were other North and South Streets in the town.

By 1846 most of the housing had been completed, although William Salmon Rolin was building in North Everard Street as late as 1850. It is clear from the outset that Everard wanted to create a development he could be proud of for he was one of the few developers to include regulatory covenants in his sale documentation. His properties are generally more spacious than those of the less regulated developments and several of them, especially those close to London Road, are of a good architectural quality.

157. 79 London Road. In 1848 this house was described as recently erected regardless of expense, probably by John Sugars.

158. North Everard Street and 5 South Everard Street, the 'round house'.

159. South Everard Street, south-east end, northern side. Nicely finished corner.

160. 20-22 North Everard Street. Good architectural composition and detailing.

161. South side of Valinger's Road.

Goodwin's Fields (Goodwin's Road etc) (13)

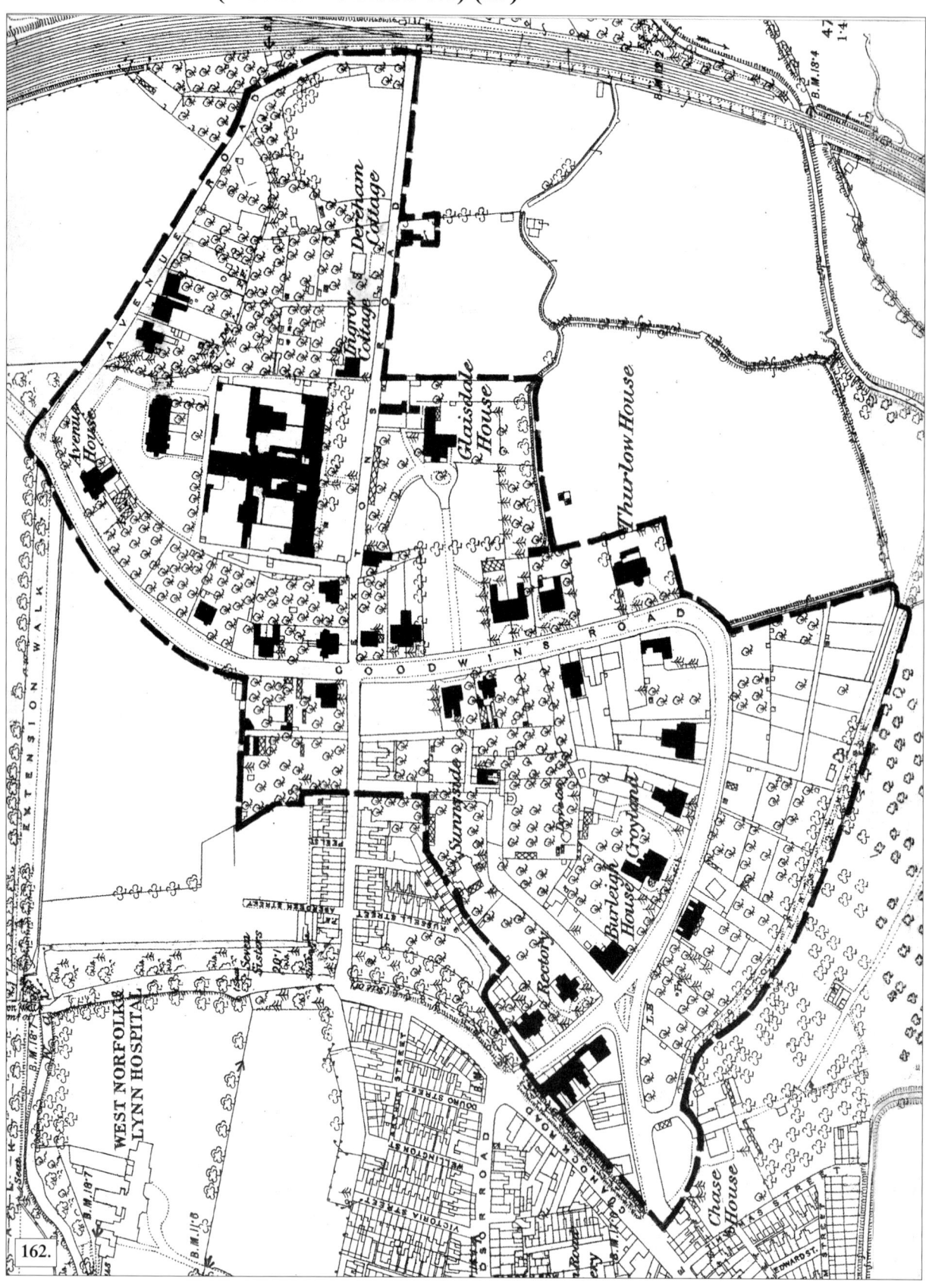

163. The Old Rectory, Goodwin's Road, built c1842.

Writing in 1891 about Dr Harvey Goodwin, John Dyker Thew commented; 'The name of his family is commemorated in that of Goodwin's road, which was made by his father (Charles), and was the first attempt to establish anything like a suburb of the town of Lynn. It long proved a failure, for the few houses first built were much unoccupied, but it has risen into greater favour of late years'. [69]

The suburb he was referring to was Charles Goodwin's third development venture in Lynn, following those at the Guanock Field and Clough Garden. Although he was soon to embark on the development of Marshall's Orchard, another low rental affair, he seems at this stage in his life to have wanted to create a garden suburb to cater for the more affluent members of Lynn Society and perhaps provide himself with a lasting memorial.

However, if he did publish a prospectus of his intentions, no copy appears to have survived, nor have the layout plans referred to in the Corporation minutes, so the story of Goodwin's Fields has to be pieced together from other sources.

In 1840 Goodwin purchased 20 acres of pasture from Candler Brown. It lay to the east of the line of the town defences, in the vicinity of the site of the Guanock Gate. In November that year he approached the Corporation for permission to create an access into this land from Guanock Terrace, but no agreement was reached. This was probably because Goodwin resisted the Corporation's demand for a fee of £500, 'in consideration of the increased value which such Road would give to the Land so purchased by Mr. Goodwin'.

A year later, in November 1841, Goodwin proposed a land exchange with the Corporation, in order to improve the viability of his holding. This the Corporation agreed to as it was seen as beneficial to its interests. Given this encouragement Goodwin finalised his proposals and in March 1842 the Advertiser carried a piece about a new suburb to be laid out adjacent to the town. This article set out the scheme's three main proposals: firstly to extend the avenue of trees in the New Walks to double its length over Saers Marsh; secondly to continue Almshouse Road (now Tennyson Avenue) over the lower part of Saer's Marsh, to emerge near the site of the Guanock Gate, close to the entrance to the Chase; and lastly to construct a new road across the land opposite the

164. Fairlight Lodge, Goodwin's Road, built c1875.

end of Windsor Road, almost in a straight line to the bridge at the end of the Chase, and thence to Hardwick Road. The journalist concluded that if these alterations were carried out 'there will be two additional entrances into the town, one from the Hardwick-road, and the other from Gaywood'.

Goodwin's plan showing these proposals, was submitted to the Corporation for approval and on 30th April 1842 it was decided that they were acceptable except for the new road to Hardwick Road. As a result a Committee was formed to settle the details with Goodwin, 'he entering into a stipulation that no Privy shall at any time be permitted to have its outlet into any of the Public Drains. And that all Houses to be erected upon Mr. Goodwin's Land shall front the Public Roads and Walks'.

On 2nd May 1842 this Committee decided to recommend the Corporation to grant Goodwin permission to construct a road, at least 40 feet wide, across Guanock Terrace, to connect to his proposed new road on payment of £200. The Corporation accepted this recommendation but Goodwin did not, protesting that he was making a public improvement

165. Plaxtole House, Goodwin's Road, built c1875.

and therefore should not have to pay for the privilege. Eventually, however, he gave way and development commenced.

It is clear from the foregoing that Goodwin intended to create a superior housing development, but with a lack of interest from both developers and tenants he was obliged to lay out and sell many of the plots as gardens and pleasure grounds. These were planted up and provided with summerhouses for enjoyment as leafy retreats away from the hurly burly of urban living.

From mid-1842 there appeared in the Advertiser a steady stream of 'villa residences' for sale or to let on this site, with the same properties changing hands at all too frequent intervals. Pleasure gardens also appeared for sale as such and as building plots. The South Lynn tithe map of 1844 shows the embryonic garden suburb with just five houses (four of them owned by Thomas Dyson), together with 13 holdings described as gardens. [70] These houses, however, were substantial properties built in gault brick and it is to be supposed that Goodwin insisted on a certain size and a standard of design in keeping with his aspirations.

166. Villas in Exton's Road, built c1860.

167. Hamilton House, Goodwin's Road, built c1860.

When in 1850 some of these early houses came up for sale their rental value ranged from £50 to £56 per annum.

On 23rd October 1852 the Advertiser reported that; 'We have experienced considerable satisfaction in witnessing the carrying out of a most desirable improvement on the out skirts of the town – to wit, the entire re-construction of the curvilinear road leading from Guanock road, nearly opposite Windsor place across the end of the Long Walk, towards Gaywood. The path has been relaid with gravel, and the road with gravel flints, of first-rate quality, on a bed of durable material;…'.

There is no evidence to suggest that this improvement accelerated the very slow rate of development of the suburb and in White's Directory of 1854 only ten people are listed as living in Goodwin's Fields.

That same year the St. James' Workhouse collapsed and the search was on for a replacement site. Three possibilities were identified namely, a piece of land on the Hardwick Road, a site in Goodwin's Fields, and land owned by Joseph Cooper on the north side of Exton's Road. The owners of the latter two were asked to state their price. After some deliberation the Board of Guardians decided to accept Cooper's offer to sell them a 3½-acre site, for £1,100.

The new workhouse was opened in 1856 on a site, which although not owned by Goodwin, was in reality part of Goodwin's Fields. It seems surprising that Goodwin entertained the idea of a workhouse within his garden suburb although he was clearly a public spirited man.

The next plan to show the suburb in any detail was that published by Thew in 1868. This bears out his earlier quoted comment for only ten more houses are shown than those depicted in 1844.

When Goodwin died in 1859 he would have been all too aware that, despite his best efforts, his project had failed. However, by the time Thew published his next plan, in 1881, a considerable number of additional houses had been built and the suburb had taken on something of the form that Goodwin had envisaged.

Since then Lynn has engulfed Goodwin's Fields and the construction of Vancouver Avenue has distorted its road layout. Its garden suburb qualities, however, are still discernible.

168. Burleigh House, Goodwin's Road, built c1875.

Marshall's Orchard (Albert Street etc) (14)

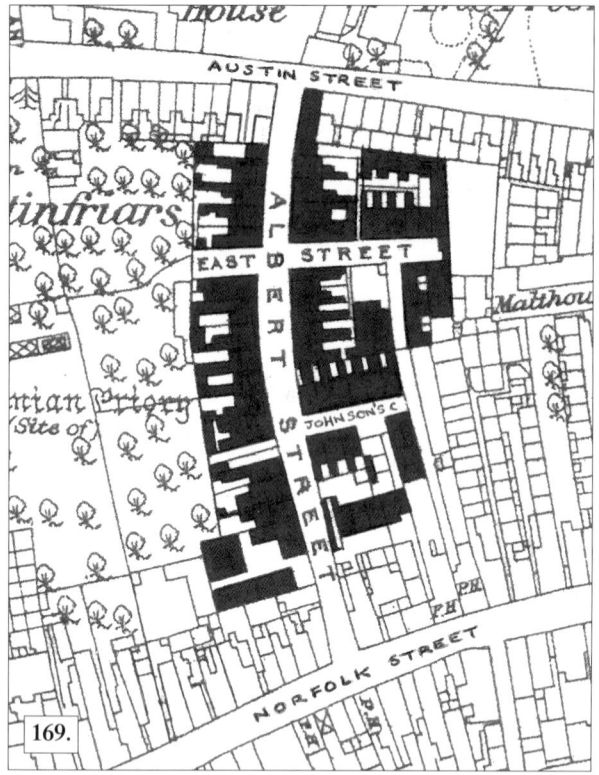

169.

On 20th June 1843 the Advertiser reported that; 'We perceive that a great improvement is being made in the formation of a new street from Austin street to Norfolk street, the latter entrance being nearly opposite Paradise-lane. This spirited alteration which is going on, under the direction of Charles Goodwin, Esq., promises great accommodation to the inhabitants, as there is no intermediate communication between the streets in question, except a contracted yard, or dirty thoroughfare. A number of houses we find are already in course of erection, and from their position and style of building, no doubt they will be found very agreeable as to their situation, and in their internal arrangements comfortable residences'.

Goodwin's latest development venture was much closer to home as it abutted the garden of his house in Chapel Street. Before he bought the land in 1840 it was an orchard owned by Thomas Marshall.

To enable him to develop, Goodwin had to create an access into the site from Austin Street. This he did by purchasing frontage property from the estate of the newly bankrupt William Newham. In a similar fashion he connected the site to Norfolk Street.

Albert Street was named after Queen Victoria's consort, Prince Albert. The other street in the development, East Street, was laid out and informally named by the end of 1843. The Paving Commissioners did not confirm this until 1855, suggesting that the houses in this small street were not built until the early 1850s. Also part of the development was Johnson's Court, which existed by 1851, as there was an application to the Paving Commissioners that year for one of the gas lamps in Albert Street to be moved, so as to light this Yard.

By January 1844 sufficient progress had been made for the 'Owners and Occupiers of Property in

170. Austin Street. Entrance to Albert Street from the north, 1967.

171. Albert Street, looking south c1965.

the newly formed Street called Albert Street and other Inhabitants of the Town' to request that the street be paved and lit by the Paving Commissioners. This was deferred because the street was not built up on both sides. By August that year, however, the Commissioners agreed to construct footways and to gravel the carriageway suggesting that by then the development of Albert Street was largely complete.

Most of the area was cleared in the late 1960s as part of the town centre redevelopment, although six houses survive on the east side of Albert Street.

172. Johnson's Court off Albert Street, c1934.

Blackfriars Pasture (Railway Road, Portland Street etc) (15)

During the early 19th Century the Bagge family owned this pasture. Until the 1840s the land was let for agricultural purposes and along its southern boundary was a ropewalk. In the south-west corner lay the remains of the Blackfriars Friary from which the pasture took its name.

William Bagge of Lynn and Gaywood died in 1835 leaving this land to his nephew Edward, who took the first tentative steps to develop it by selling plots along the frontage to North Clough Lane (which, after the completion of the Purfleet scheme, was renamed Blackfriars Street). The first building to be constructed was the Stepney Baptist Chapel, which was opened for worship in 1841. Other buildings followed and in 1843 the Temperance Hall and Hotel were built to the east of the small access strip that had been left opposite St. James' Road, on the line of the future Railway Road.

In 1844 Edward Bagge became involved in the Lynn and Ely Railway Company's proposal to site its terminus on this pasture, but the following year he died leaving his brother and heir, Richard, to complete the sale of the necessary land and to develop the remainder.

As has already been mentioned, the railway company wanted to close the Echo Road and construct a new link to connect London Road to Norfolk Street. The station was to be sited on the eastern side of this link. In the event the new street was laid out, but the railway company decided to build a temporary station on the Echo Road, intending to build a permanent one further forward

174. The Stepney Baptist Chapel, Blackfriars Street, built in 1841.

at a later date. In 1849, however, this idea was abandoned.

On 7th September 1846 the Paving Commissioners named the new street Railway Road, but it was already being referred to as Station Street in anticipation of the arrival of the station. It continued to be variously called Station Street, Station Road, and Railway Street until December 1857 when the Paving Commissioners were asked to settle the matter. The clerk pronounced that it was 'termed most generally Railway Road'.

The Commissioners adopted the road as early as August 1846, but in 1847, when they considered a request by the railway company to undertake its repair, they replied that 'as the said Road is not yet formed into a Street by the Erection of a continuous line of Buildings on each side of it, the Commissioners do not at a present feel called upon to undertake to repair it'.

By April 1847 houses had been built on Railway Road and it is to be presumed that these stood on the western side, on Bagge land, as the whole of the pasture on the eastern side was still owned by the railway company. But in 1849, having made the decision not to build another station, the company declared this land surplus to requirements and it was put up for sale by auction.

The sale particulars were published in the Advertiser on 12th May 1849 and a surviving plan shows the land divided into 14 lots arranged around a framework of three streets, North, Middle, and South. 71 In the event many of these lots failed to sell but William Smith Simpson, the railway contractor, bought those on both sides of Middle Street, either directly or from Henry Barnett. On this land he built the East Anglian Hotel, and two substantial terraces of houses fronting the road, which he renamed Portland Street. His aim was to create a prestigious approach to the station, which at that time stood opposite the eastern end of his street.

On 25th November 1850 the Paving Commissioners confirmed the name Portland Street and Smith Simpson set about marketing his houses but, with no one willing to buy, he was forced to let them.

Most of the remaining land was sold to Henry Barnett of Lombard Street, London. Over the ensuing years he tried to market it for development but with little success. He owned land on both sides of what were then known as North Portland Street and South Portland Street. In November 1852, against the owner's wishes, the Paving Commissioners renamed these streets Wellesley

175. Railway Road, eastern side, looking north. Note the prominent entrance to Portland Street.

Street and Waterloo Street, further honouring the Duke of Wellington.

There was some house building in these streets but the major part of the land was not developed for that purpose. The north side of Wellesley Street was laid out as cattle pens for the railway, after being advertised as mercantile sites in 1856.

When the Bagges sold the eastern half of the pasture to the railway company, they retained the southern frontage to Blackfriars Road. In 1850 Richard Bagge sold this land to William Salmon Rolin, who built St. John's Terrace on it.

On 16th March 1850 the Advertiser referred to this land as, 'about to be covered with a line of new buildings, which, we are informed, will be of an ornamental character'. From the poor rate records it

176. Waterloo Street, north side from the west, c1965.

is possible to established the manner in which Rolin built the terrace. Nos 1-4, at the western end, were completed and let in 1851. At the other end, 10-14 were built in 1852. The middle section, Nos 5-9, was not built until 1853-54 and this is marked by a slight forward projection and a change in balcony decoration. Rolin built No 14, now the Belgrave Hotel, for himself. [72]

177. Portland Street, north side, looking west, c1965.

Richard Bagge had retained the remainder of the pasture west of Railway Road and now set about developing it. By early 1850 he had laid out Market Street, which was named on 6th May 1850 and Albion Street, which was not formally named until November 1854. He then sold off plots to various builders, including William Johnson, Robert Mott, Simon Ockley, James Purdy and Edward Walker.

178. The East Anglian Hotel, Blackfriars Road, 1965.

One of the last plots to be sold was the site of the Union Baptist Chapel, which was opened in 1859. This building is now the Lynn Museum.

Today all the development to the east of Railway Road remains intact apart from the bomb damaged western end of St. John's Terrace. The development to the west, however, has not fared so well, with much of Market Street and Albion Street being cleared in the 1960s as part of the town centre redevelopment.

179. St. John's Terrace, Blackfriars Road, c1930.

The Brickyard (Exton's Road etc) (16)

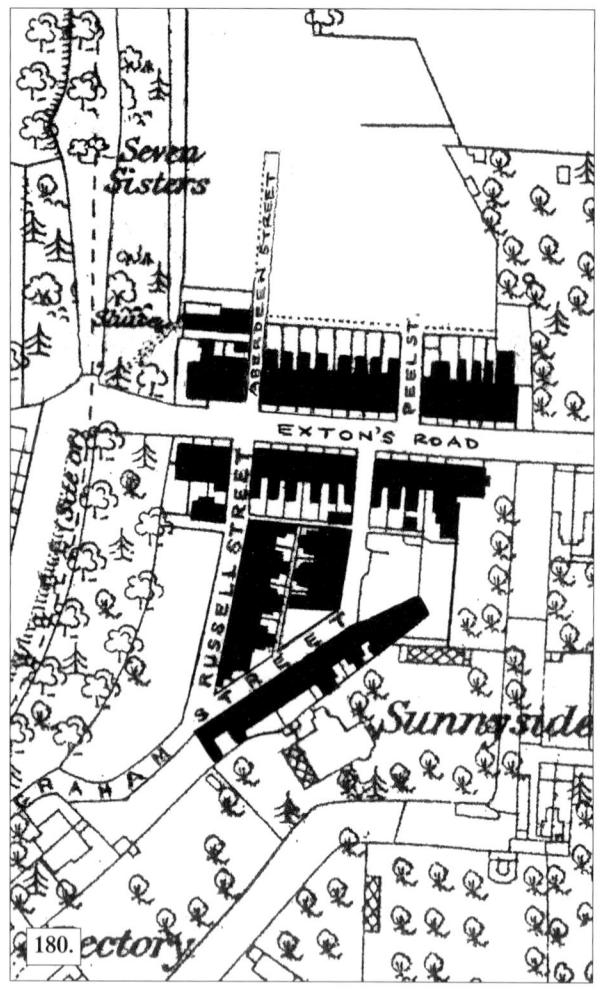

180.

Until renamed in 1850 Exton's Road was called Brick Kiln Road, reflecting the fact that it served two brick-making sites. The South Lynn Tithe Map of 1844 shows that the one nearest the town occupied the site of a bastion constructed shortly after the Siege of Lynn, in 1643.[73] It was owned and occupied by Samuel Page.

On 28th October 1848 the Advertiser carried a notice concerning the sale by auction of 'About **Three Acres** and a half of **Freehold Land**, suitable for Building purposes, containing a good depth of Brick Earth, having been hitherto used as a Brick field, with a small Cottage, Kiln and Sheds… situate…, near the Public Walks'. Particulars were to be obtained from John Sugars.

The land was bought by William Salmon Rolin, who initially continued working the site as a brickyard, possibly making bricks for his own use. In the 1851 census he is described as employing six brickmakers, but that year he decided to develop the site for housing.

As with most things Rolin did there were complications. In June 1851 he applied to the Corporation for permission to tunnel the ditch, which separated his site from the Terrace Walk, in order to improve the value of his land, but the application was turned down. Undaunted he set about laying out streets and sub-dividing the site into plots to be built on by him and other builders.

Work progressed but he was soon in trouble with the Paving Commissioners over non-compliance with the building regulations. In May 1852 he was charged at the magistrates court with having 'built, or begun to build the same (four cottages near Exton's Road) without partition walls, wholly of brick or stone, and of the thickness of nine inches and also without notice previously given to the surveyor to the Commissioners, contrary to the Paving Act'.

After expressing a wish that the case should be heard by disinterested parties, i.e. magistrates who were not Paving Commissioners, he admitted that the party walls were only 4½ inches thick, but that he was of the opinion that the jurisdiction of the Paving Commissioners did not apply east of the

181. Exton's Road, north side.

108

Guanock Gate, where the land was considered to be in the rural part of the Borough. In the event his defence was not accepted but the case was dismissed because the complaint had not been made within the prescribed period of two months from the committal of the offence.

182. Russell Street from the west.

Rolin was unchastened by this for in December 1852 the Commissioners' surveyor reported the erection of houses in Exton's Road by Messrs Rolin, Ockley and Turner in which the provisions of the Act had been ignored. The clerk was directed to serve formal notices on the men to remedy the situation.

At a meeting of the Paving Commissioners held on 5th January 1853, Rolin again had to defend a case of non-compliance concerning the site but, bizarrely, at the same time he made a request for pavements to be constructed in South Everard Street and in front of his St. John's Terrace development. The Advertiser report of the meeting also mentioned that; 'A letter was received from Messrs Goodwin & Co., with a tracing of the plan of some new streets on Mr. Rolin's land, adjoining Exton's road, the names proposed for which included "Aberdeen Street", "Peel Street", "Russell Street", Etc'. [74] The reporter went on to comment that; 'Some little risability was excited, in the course of the debate which followed'. The other name agreed for this development was Graham Street. All four commemorated prominent politicians, three of them recent prime ministers, but the fact that this provoked a degree of mirth is more likely to do with the Commissioners' opinion of Rolin than the choice of names.

With the housing market starting to wane, development of these streets proceeded slowly. In December 1853 the property of one of Rolin's co-builders, Simon Ockley, was auctioned, as he had been declared a bankrupt. This included two cottages on the north side of Exton's Road and six in Graham Street. In October 1854 Rolin himself went bankrupt and the development of the site was suddenly halted.

Peel Street and Aberdeen Street were never developed leaving them as streets in name only. Further development did take place, however, in the 1870s in Graham Street and on the east side of Russell Street.

The area today is largely intact except for the south-east side of Graham Street which has suffered demolition. The unfinished streets bear testimony to the collapse of house building in Lynn in the mid-1850s.

183. Peel Street. 'A road to nowhere'.

Lower Canada (Coburg Street etc) (17)

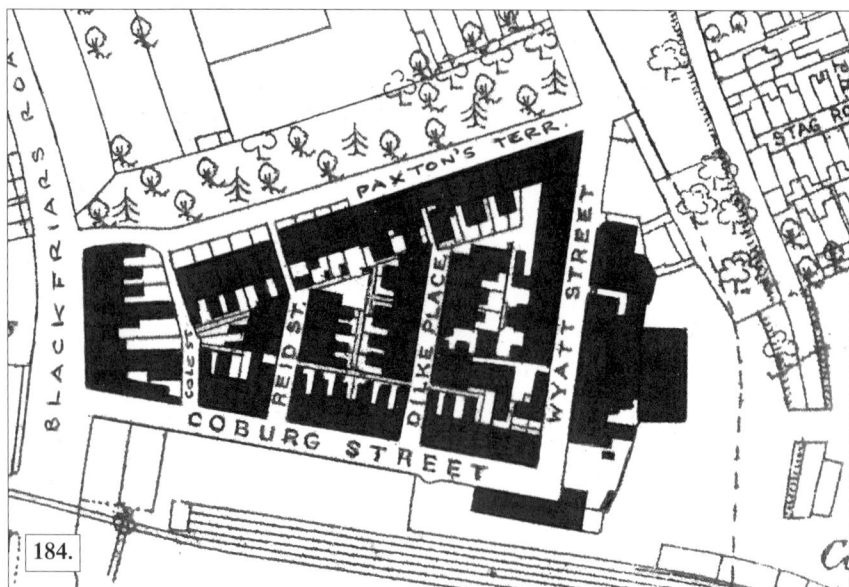

184.

Of all the development that took place at this time, it was Lower Canada which attracted most contemporary criticism. Armes commented that; 'Of course I need not speak of matters so familiar, even to the youth of the present day, as the alterations about the railway station, and the erections in what is popularly called *Lower Canada*, a site too low, by the way, for habitable dwellings except in so far as they put money into the pockets of some speculators or mortgagees'. [75]

Furthermore at the Council Meeting held on 31st October 1857, there was a discussion about the desirability of constructing a bridge over the Pierrepoint Drain into Chase Road. Concern was expressed about the possibility of this opening up land for 'a lot of little dirty cottages'. Mr. Creswell, who made this comment, went on to say; 'They had an instance of the kind in "Lower Canada". Who would ever have supposed that people would go to build there? It was a great detriment to the town,…'.

The site of Lower Canada originally formed part of a much larger field, which was bought by the railway company from the Corporation. In 1847 it became the property of the East Anglian Railway Company, which had taken over the local lines. By late 1849 a number of pieces of land had been identified as surplus to railway requirements and on 7th November several were sold to Charles Henry Holman of Milverton in Somerset. This included the piece on which Lower Canada was to be built. In 1851 Holman sold this for £810 to a consortium comprising shoemaker, William Miles, merchant James Wright and builder Robert Mott.

185. Coburg Street, looking west, c1965.

Mott was also an auctioneer and the sale documentation stated that he 'should soon after sell and dispose of the sd pieces of land either together or in parcels either by Public Auction or private contract or partly by each for the best prices that could be reasonably gotten...'. [76] The money so received was to be shared equally between them.

Mott was required to lay out streets and sewers. This he did with the aid of local architects Cruso & Maberley who set out on a plan the street layout and blocks of building land. In all 28 blocks were sold to a variety of builders and investors.

The Great Exhibition was held in 1851 and this provided Mott and his associates with the inspiration for street names. On 21st June the Advertiser carried a piece stating that the Exhibition, 'has already stamped its impress upon our town, the principal persons connected with this undertaking having already given names to several new streets, laid out in a tract of building land near the railway terminus. The princely founder of the work gives his title to "Coburg Street" - the Secretary to the Royal Commissioners will live on in "Wyatt Street", – the Executive triumvirate are respectively to be remembered in "Reid Street", "Dilke Street", and "Cole Street" – and he who has, with such wonderful ingenuity housed the mighty congress, will find a memento in "Paxton Terrace" '.

186. Wyatt Street from the south-east, c1965.

These names were not confirmed by the Paving Commissioners until 20th March 1852 when possibly the earliest reference to Lower Canada appears, a name which so far has defied satisfactory explanation.

Virtually nothing remains of this area, it being demolished in the 1960s under slum clearance procedures.

187. Dilke Street, looking north, c1965.

188. Reid Street, looking north, c1965.

111

EPILOGUE

With the collapse of house building in the mid 1850s and the completion of the Paving Commissioners' last major project in 1866, the remaking of King's Lynn, as defined in this book, came to a close.

In a little over six decades the appearance of the

189. The Alexandra Dock, 1871. Watercolour by William Austin.

town had dramatically changed. The mediaeval streets of 1800 had been transformed into modern Georgian thoroughfares and the number of houses had doubled, with most of the new ones occupying the space between the old built up area and the line of the town defences.

That there was little adverse reaction to this metamorphosis was due largely to the fact that the Georgian architecture, which characterised the new and refronted buildings, had steadily been making its presence felt in the town since the early 18th century, when it was first established by, amongst others, Henry Bell. Its adoption was seen as progress, indeed something to aspire to rather than bemoan. There was no widespread nostalgia for what had gone.

From 1866 until the end of the 19th Century, the area within the town defences remained largely undisturbed. What development there was in the town took place beyond that line and this included further improvement to the town's infrastructure, such as the expansion of the rail network and the construction, in the old Ouse Channel, of the Alexandra Dock (1869) and the Bentinck Dock (1884).

The establishment and expansion of the engineering works of Frederick Savage, Alfred Dodman, and Cooper Roller Bearings provided some much needed manufacturing employment and gradually Lynn began to recover from the slump brought about by the introduction of the national rail network. It was not, however, until 1901 that the town's recorded population exceeded that of the heady days of 1851.

The first significant change to the form and character of the old town was the filling in of the Millfleet in 1898.

The First World War was the next event to impact on the appearance of the town. On 19th January 1915 two Zeppelins crossed the North Sea and dropped bombs on Great Yarmouth, Sheringham, and King's Lynn. This was the first air raid to be inflicted on this country. In Lynn, East Street and Bentinck Street bore the brunt of the damage.

In the early 1930s it was the turn of the Yards to feel the cold wind of change. The indisputable insanitary conditions that existed there had long been a source of complaint and various attempts had been made to persuade the Corporation to deal with the problem by carrying out slum clearance.

190. East Street after the Zeppelin raid of 19th January 1915.

191. St. John's Terrace. House built in the 1950s on the site of Nos 1-2 which were destroyed by enemy action.

To provide the necessary information, public health officers inspected the Yards and pronounced every house unfit for human habitation. As a result the Corporation formed a Slum Clearance Committee, which put forward proposals to the Council on 2nd August 1933. Plans were drawn up for the provision of new housing for those living in the yards and the yards themselves were pulled down. Their passing went unlamented but fortunately a photographic record was taken. [77]

The Second World War brought with it renewed efforts to destroy the town from the air with sadly 57 civilians being killed. On 13th November 1940 a lone German raider dropped a stick of 19 high explosive bombs, which fell across London Road, Valinger's Road, Friar Street, and Ethel Terrace. Seven days later another aircraft dropped bombs in a line from St. John's Terrace to South Street, demolishing properties in both these streets and in Wood Street. In architectural terms the most damage was done to the integrity of St. John's Terrace, with the destruction of two houses at the western end of Rolin's imposing creation.

A further raid on 12th June 1941 destroyed Boal Street and caused serious damage in Bridge Street, whilst that on 12th June 1942 scored a direct hit on the Eagle Hotel in Norfolk Street, causing much loss of life.

After the war the gaps created by the bombing were filled and in the 1950s the old town looked much the same as it had in 1870, save for the disappearance of the Yards. This was all about to change.

At the time the town largely depended on agriculturally related employment, a sector where the wage rates were notoriously low. This forced many youngsters to leave the town in search of better paid jobs, a trend the Borough Council was keen to arrest.

In 1958 it managed to attract Campbell's Soups to a site on Hardwick Road and Dow Chemicals came to the town shortly afterwards. Although the products from these companies related to agriculture, their successful introduction encouraged the Council to seek 'expanded town' status under the provisions of the Town Development Act, 1952. In 1962 an agreement was signed with the then London County Council to expand the town by taking London overspill.

It was realised that if the scheme was to be successful, the existing town would have to be modernised, especially the town centre, which would need a range of shops and facilities to match the newcomers' expectations.

In 1963 a development plan was drawn up setting out areas for housing and industry, together with a new road network. In addition, plans were laid for a modern town centre, incorporating pedestrianised streets, car parks, service roads, a bus station, and a number of supermarkets; in effect a second

192. Campbell's Soup factory, established in the town in 1958.

remaking of Lynn. But, unlike the first, its impact was so immediate and drastic that the dismay felt by many still reverberates today.

The fact that the proposals would require large scale demolition of the old town were sufficiently understood to prompt the setting up of the King's Lynn Archaeological Survey and the commissioning by Norfolk County Council and the King's Lynn Borough Council of a joint report to consider the impact of the proposals on the historic area. Produced in 1964, this was entitled, 'The Historic Core of King's Lynn – A Study and Plan', and is

193. Out with the old in with the new. Hillington Square January 1968.

usually referred to as the Chesterton Report after its author, Dame Elizabeth Chesterton.

Its recommendations caused some of the town centre proposals to be modified but, at a time when the concept of conservation had yet to reach the statute book, the emphasis for preservation was placed on what was termed the historic core, i.e. the waterfront streets from the Tuesday Market Place to Nelson Street.

This implied that the remainder of the old town was of little consequence clearing the way for whole streets of historic buildings to be demolished or partially destroyed to make way for the new facilities. These streets included North Street, Pilot Street, Austin Street, St. Nicholas Street, Chapel Street, Surrey Street, Purfleet Street, New Conduit Street, Sedgeford Lane, Broad Street, Baker Lane, and Church Street. As a result, a significant proportion of the property which had been remodelled by the Paving Commissioners disappeared, together with much that had survived from earlier times.

The 19th century housing developments were not immune from this process either, although it has to be said that many had never risen above their speculative origins and by the 1960s were ready for clearance. In this way Dixon's Garden, Middleton's Meadow, Ffolkes' Garden, Marshall's Garden, Cade's Garden, Highgate, Kirby's Ground, Clough Garden, Marshall's Orchard, and Lower Canada were totally or partially demolished.

Across the country this wholesale destruction of historic towns, to provide for car-based modern living, provoked an outcry from those with an appreciation of historic buildings and townscapes. This led to the creation of conservation areas under the Civic Amenities Act 1967.

A conservation area for Lynn was designated as early as 1969, but this only included the previously identified historic core, and therefore served to reinforce the view that the remainder of the old town was of little importance thereby, if anything, accelerating the process of demolition.

By the early 1970s the town centre had largely been redeveloped, but the downturn in the economy caused by the oil crisis brought the process to a halt before the new could be fully integrated with the old. This period of respite, however, enabled the Conservation Area to be expanded in 1979 to include all that remained of the old town. Now protected, its future looks secure.

By contrast the town centre, which displaced a large area of the old town, has recently been refronted or rebuilt but in a style which is still out of keeping with the familiar and cherished character of the old town, arguably Lynn's greatest asset.

APPENDIX

The Street Names of King's Lynn before and after the re-naming of 1809.

Before	After
St. James's Street and Three Pidgeon Street to the White Hart Inn inclusive	St. James' Street
Grass Market & Dampgate Street to Littleport Bridge	Norfolk Street
Littleport Street	Littleport Street
Littleport Bridge	Littleport Bridge
Bridge near the Site of the East Gate	East Gate Bridge
King Staith Yard	King Staith Square
Lane next W Swatman's House	King Staith Lane
Broad Street	Broad Street
Lath Street	Nelson Street
Street leading from Black Goose Street to the Fort	St Ann Street
Black Horse Street	Chapel Street
Black Goose Street	St. Nicholas Street
Fisher Bridge	North Bridge
Row beyond Fisher Bridge	North End
Cross Lane in Hopman's Lane to the Chapel	Chapel Lane
From Chapel Lane to Fisher Bridge	Pilot Street
Dog Street	North Street
Hopman's Lane	Austin Street
Pagestair Lane	Pagestair Lane
Pudding Lane	Water Lane
Common Staithe Lane	Ferry Street
Chequer Street	King Street
Purfleet Bridge	Purfleet Bridge
Purfleet Street	Purfleet Street
Purfleet Quay	Purfleet Quay
High Street from the Tuesday Market Place to the Saturday Market Place	High Street
Duke's Head Lane	Market Lane
Butcher Lane	Jews Lane
New Conduit Street	New Conduit Street
The Plain	The Plain
Baxter's Bridge	Baxter's Bridge
Saint Margarets Lane	St Margarets Lane
Spinner Lane	Paradise Lane
North Clough Lane	North Clough Lane
South Clough Lane	South Clough Lane
Sedgeford Lane	Sedgeford Lane
Black Boy Street	Tower Street
Codlin Lane	Tower Lane
Mill Lane	Stonegate
Red Cow Street	Church Street
Priory Lane	Priory Lane
From College Lane to Saint Margarets Lane	St Margaret's Place

From the Guildhall inclusive to the White Hart Inn	Saturday Market
Three Crown Street	Queen Street
Street from Lady Bridge Southward to Mr. Nurse's House	Bridge Street
Passage from Mr. Nurse's House to the Friars	White Friars Gate
Baker Lane	Baker Lane
From the Wrestlers Public House to the King Staith Yard	Purfleet Place
Mad Lane	Union Lane
Cross Lane	Cross Lane
College Lane	College Lane
Street from Mr. Nurse's House to South Lynn Plain	All Saints Street
Street from the South Gate to the Dolphin Public House	Southgate Street
Street from the Dolphin Public House to South Lynn Plain	Friars Street
From Valinger's Hospital to the New Road	Valinger's Road
New Road	London Road
South Lynn Plain	South Lynn Plain
Crooked Lane	Crooked Lane
Lane between Mr. Day's and Mr. Pursglove's Estates	Ouse Lane
Lane between the Estates late Mr. Partridge's & Mr. Silverwood's	River Lane
Lane next Mr. Thos Allen's House	Ship Lane
Street leading from Bridge Street to the Boal	Boal Street
Lane leading from South Lynn Plain	Church Lane

Source: Borough Archives KL/PC2/2

Sources

The main documentary source for this work has been the King's Lynn Borough Archives. The relevant documents are:-

Paving Commissioners

i   Committee Minutes, KL/PC1/1 (1790-1803,1806)

ii   Commissioners' Minutes, KL/PC2/1 (1803-06), 2 (1806-15), 3 (1815-23), 4 (1823-30), 5 (1830-44), 6 (1844-51), 7 (1851-58), 8 (1859-66), 9 (1866-72), together with the Minutes of the Urban Sanitary Authority (1872-3).

iii   Commissioners' Accounts, KL/PC3/1 (1803-1827)

iv   KL/PC unnumbered papers

v   Paving Acts 1803,1806,1859

Corporation

i   Hall Books, KL/C7/- especially 15 (1786-1822), 16 (1822-1847), 17 (1848-1864)

ii   Committee Minutes, KL/TC2/1/-, especially 1 (1793-1820), 2 (1820-1835), 3 (1835-1851)

iii   Chamberlain's Accounts, KL/C39/-

iv   Enrolled Private Deeds, KL/C11/-, especially 20 (1803-10), 21 (1810-17), 22 (1817-24), 23 (1824-30), 24 (1831-38), 25 (1839-45), 26 (1845-57)

v   Quarter Sessions, Minutes KL/C20/-

Other sources include miscellaneous private deeds, the Lynn Advertiser (from 1842), sales particulars, census reports, and trade directories.

Less frequently used primary sources are referred to in the Notes and References.

Secondary sources are listed in the Bibliography.

Notes and References

1. In 1962 the Society for Mediaeval Archaeology held its fifth conference in King's Lynn and this led to the formation, in 1963, of the Survey, under the able chairmanship of Professor Eleanora Carus-Wilson. Its work led to three publications: Vanessa Parker (1971), Helen Clarke and Alan Carter (1977), and Dorothy Owen (1984).

2. For the purposes of this study, the 'old town' comprises the streets and pre-1870 buildings, which lie between the river and the line of the former town defences.

3. Owen, p9

4. Defoe, p96

5. In the preface to their book, the Webbs commented that 'the Improvement Commissioners have not previously been made the subject of historical study'. This they rectified, but since then the topic has received scant attention, especially in respect of individual towns.

6. NRO. BL42/1. This Plan provides an invaluable snapshot of the improvements that had been carried out between May 1803 and February 1806. It shows much that is impossible to glean from the written sources.

7. White's Directory, 1836, p390

8. John James Coulton (1818-1908) was the son of an attorney of the same name, who had a practice in Austin Street. His father was appointed Clerk to the Paving Commissioners in 1814, a post he held until his death in 1840, when Coulton, at the age of 22, succeeded him. He remained their Clerk until the disbandment of the Commissioners in 1872. It is noticeable that from 1840 the Commissioners' Minutes become more informative.
Inheriting his father's practice, Coulton went into partnership with Edward Milligan Beloe and acquired the clerkship to the Board of Guardians and that to the Turnpike Trustees. He also became the Superintendent Registrar and Deputy Coroner and therefore was well placed to comment on Lynn's nineteenth century era of town expansion. His recollections on this subject and much more appeared in the Lynn Advertiser in 1880.

9. There are three dated examples: 25 Queen Street (1812), 49/50 High Street (1830), and 19 King Street (1827).

10. W Richards, Vol II. p1213

11. Thew said of Sheppard, 'He was an intelligent man, and I think served the town as a member of the Hospital Board. Eventually the fortune he had acquired as a tailor was dissipated in brickmaking, building, and other speculations'. (Thew, p50).

12. The current Saturday Market Place was originally part of the churchyard of St. Margaret's. As late as 1765 a new wall was built to enclose this area, but this had gone by the time the Commissioners set about reducing the spread of the market.

13. A detailed plan of the Sexton's House and its relationship to the Church in 1772 is to be found in NRO. Colman Col/7/12

14. Francis Goodwin (1784-1835) was the son of Lynn attorney, Harvey Goodwin, and brother of Charles Goodwin, who figures prominently in the town expansion section of this book. He was a pupil of the architect J. Coxedge of Kensington and later became an assistant to John Walters. By the mid-1820s he had a successful practice in the Midlands and was responsible for a number of municipal buildings, including Manchester Town Hall. Between 1820 and 1830 he designed and built 14 churches largely in the late Gothic style. He also had a penchant for entering design competitions, including that for the new Houses of Parliament, the concentration on which caused him to have apoplexy from which he died. Apart from the Trinity Chapel and other minor Lynn works, Goodwin is best known locally for his publication, 'A Narrative of the Grand Festival Given by the Inhabitants of King's Lynn on Friday the 22nd of July 1814', and the large engraving of the dinner held on that occasion in the Tuesday Market Place.

15. Initially the Committee decided to employ the Norwich School artist Robert Dixon to paint a one-act scene, perhaps because he had already worked in Lynn as an artist. However, there was a misunderstanding, probably caused by William Newham, and as a result all the scene painting was given to a Mr. Whitmore of Covent Garden.

16. William Newham (1776-1858) is a prominent character in this story. Thew recalled; 'I remember Mr. Newham, a builder in a large way of business, an able man but not very refined in his conversation. He had extensive shops and premises at the North End'. (Thew p53).

    He was the son of the architect/builder Samuel Newham, who was the Paving Commissioners' first surveyor until his death in 1816. He is probably the same William Newham who became a pupil of James Wyatt, exhibiting two architectural designs at the Royal Academy in 1796/7. In 1804 he was appointed Town Chamberlain, but was dismissed in 1816 because of his conduct in relation to the theatre. It caused him to be declared bankrupt, but fortunately for him, that same year he inherited his father's business. By then he had built the Trinity Chapel and the theatre, but despite his efforts to become involved in projects such as the new Market House, he did not receive any more public commissions in Lynn.

    He was also a surveyor, producing the 1806 Paving Commissioners Plan and the 1809 Corporation Estate Plan. In 1839, however, he was once more declared bankrupt and his property, including his house and yard in Pilot Street, was bought by Charles Goodwin. As a result he moved into a house in London Road.

    He seems never to have recovered from this for in 1850 there was a public appeal in Lynn for '…Mr.. NEWHAM, of this Parish, architect and surveyor, who through the falling off of business of late years, is now destitute of any means to support himself and his wife…,' (Lynn Advertiser 30th Nov 1850). He had a son named William, who also became an architect, making it difficult to ascribe known work to one or the other with any degree of certainty after 1830.

17. This resolution is explained in the North End (17) section.

18. W Richards, Vol II, p1213

19. NRO. BL14/37.

20. The name of this inn is generally thought to be

a reference to Jack Crawford, who was called the 'Valiant Sailor' following his exploits at the Battle of Camperdown in 1797. Research by Roger Harrison, however, has shown that it had this name as early as 1728.

21. NRO. BL14/46
22. NRO. Church Commissioners' Map 11908
23. Lynn Advertiser 22nd June 1844
24. Robert Pursglove was a man to whom both William Richards and William Armes devoted a significant number of words. Both made it clear that he was an eccentric miser who let his home fall into a state of disrepair. A passage from Armes will suffice to give the flavour and describe the house that previously stood on the site of the vicarage. 'If we step for a moment to St. Margaret's and front the modern house of Mr. Dawber, we can well remember that upon that spot stood a large gloomy building, called in modern phrase, "Old Porsley's house". All towns at that period had haunted houses, and this was the haunted house of Lynn. Dull and bleak and heavy in style, with old leaded windows, every square of glass in which was broken long, long ago. No paint had been put upon that front for many, many a year. It had an open court entrance paved with square flagstones, which was quite covered with green moss, upon which was superadded the long grass, the growth of many years, that forced its way upwards through the space between the stones. Well, amidst all this desolation, here still lived old Porsley, a reputed miser!'
25. Survey, Borough Archives KL/C48/2; drawing, King's Lynn Museums; rebuilding, Borough Archives KL/C7/14
26. Borough Archives KL/C49/12
27. Lynn Advertiser, 4th July 1857
28. Lee, p15
29. Borough Archives, KL/PC6/6. Coulton made reference to this event in the following terms; 'The widening of the south corner of Purfleet street and High street brought to light a very curious building, the existence of which was previously not generally known. It was a vault with a beautiful groined roof, supported by a central pillar. Unfortunately the crown of the roof projected two or three feet above the level of the street so that it was necessary to destroy the building or to leave the entrance to Purfleet street pretty much as it was. A battle between taste and convenience is fought on unequal terms. In this case convenience won in a canter. The stones of the groined roof were used as rubbish to fill up the vault, and few who patronize the new Coffee Tavern know that they walk over a buried architectural gem'.
30. Colin Barton's well researched study together with the photographs published by Bob Booth provide a comprehensive record of the Lynn Yards.
31. W Richards, Vol II, p1164
32. This is not wholly conclusive, however, for the Yard names were not painted up at each entrance until 1818. This probably fixed them as those in common usage at that time, but earlier names could well now be lost.
33. Municipal Boundary Report
34. Borough Archives, KL/PC unnumbered. Petition against the Bill for the Second Paving Act. The petitioners were concerned that the land opened up by the New Road was not rateable at all under the existing Act, nor proposed to be rated by the Bill, despite having an increased value as a result of public expenditure of at least £4,000.
35. Armes: Lynn Advertiser, 24th February 1872
36. Thomas Marshall (1773-1849) was a gardener and seedsman, who ran his business from Purfleet Street. Armes recorded that his 'property was accumulated by early purchases of such plots as afterwards became valuable building land'. This was indeed the case and his will shows him to have owned substantial property in King's Lynn, South Lynn, Gaywood, the Wiggenhall's, and Colchester.
37. William Ayre became a Freeman of Lynn in 1797/8 by virtue of being an apprentice of merchant, Thomas Blackburne. In 1822 he is

described as a miller at Castle Rising and a merchant in Southgate Street Lynn. In 1827 he was stripped of the Freedom of the Borough because he had fraudulently tried to obtain the same status for Francis Kirby Reynolds by providing a false indenture of apprenticeship.

38. Charles Goodwin (1791-1859) was son of Lynn attorney, Harvey Goodwin. On the latter's death, in 1819, Charles succeeded him in the family practice and took on a number of partners, including Frederick Partridge and John Williams. In addition to his legal work, he was a property developer in Lynn and elsewhere. His firm was also involved in promoting Lynn's railways, although the activities of Williams in relation to this work were later to cause major problems for the practice, but not until after Charles' death. Generally supportive of the interests of the town, he served as a Borough Councillor between 1835 and 1855 and made significant donations to projects such as St. John's Church.

39. Municipal Boundary Report

40. Richard Checker (1777-1848) and John Checker (d1838) were brothers. In Pigot's Directory of 1822, Richard is described as a currier living in Norfolk Street. Both were heavily involved in Lynn's town expansion era and did sufficiently well to describe themselves as gentlemen in their wills. When John died he owned land in West Winch, Clenchwarton, and South Lynn and property in the High Street, Coronation Square, Norfolk Street, Baxter's Plain, Tuesday Market Place, London Road, and Checker Street. Ten years later Richard died with a similar level of wealth.

41. These were Francis Begley, Maria Gathergood, Richard Checker, John Sugars, and William Newham. In 1836 William Ayre was living at 18 Buckingham Terrace.

42. Aikin, p1

43. Burnet, pp13, 14, 46

44. William Smith Simpson (1801-1868) was a farmer and railway contractor but he also tried his hand at property development. Other than being involved with sections of the Lynn - Ely and Lynn - Dereham railways, he constructed the branch line to Wisbech and the Lynn and Hunstanton and West Norfolk lines. In 1846 he was described as of Little Downham, near Ely. In the 1850s and 60s he lived in King Street and was a Paving Commissioner between 1852 and 1864.

45. John Sugars (1804-1885) was the son of another John and both father and son feature prominently in the town expansion era, building many houses in South Lynn, especially on London Road.
In 1849 John, the son, retired from building to pursue other interests. He was elected a Borough Councillor for the North Ward in 1853 and remained on the Council until 1862. By 1851 he had become a ship owner in partnership with Francis Reed Wilson and in March 1853 their barque, the John Sugars, was launched at Monkwearmouth for the Australian trade. Following the bankruptcy of his protégé, William Salmon Rolin, Sugars seems to have taken over his shipyard, but by 1861 had retired to Hackney. He was still there in 1881 but was living in Hastings when he died in 1885. Sugars was a charitable man. At Christmas each year he distributed a gift of coal to the poor widows of South Lynn and in 1861 he placed a stain-glassed window in All Saints Church. His lasting memorial, however, is the Sugars Almshouses in Goodwin's Road, which he paid for and endowed. These were built in 1887.

46. Richard Bagge (1810-1891) was the member of this prominent merchant family most involved in the expansion of Lynn through his ownership of the Blackfriars Pasture. He lived in Gaywood Hall and also had a house in the Tuesday Market Place. He was prominent in local politics being a Borough Councillor from 1853 and twice Mayor.

47. Coulton, p1

48. Lee, p56

49. Lee, p71

50. Borough Archives, KL/TC Deeds, Albion

51. Borough Archives, KL/TC Deeds, Blackfriars Street
52. NRO. NRS14830, 29E3
53. Although there are some original railings, many of those that can be seen today are late 1980s replacements facilitated by grant aid from the Borough Council.
54. These papers were printed in the Lynn Advertiser of 24th February 1872 and subsequent issues.
55. Armes. Lynn Advertiser, 2nd March 1872
56. In 1851 Chadwick published an account of the old vicarage.
57. Armes. Lynn Advertiser, 24th February 1872
58. Borough Archives, KL/TC Deeds, Wood Street
59. Armes causes some confusion over the names of the parcels of land that Buckingham Terrace and Checker Street were built on. Giles Haycock, the owner, sold the latter to Checker and Jarvis and this I have termed Haycock's Ground for that reason. Armes calls the other piece variously Haycocks Pasture and Haycock's Field and describes it as being occupied by Haycock. It seems he rented it from the Quakers for up until Buckingham Terrace was completed he was paying to them £45-£50 rent, although for what is not specified. Armes records that the Buckingham Terrace site was used in 1814 to host South Lynn's commemoration of the peace of that year. 'I was a boy then, but I have memories never to be effaced of huge puddings, heavy joints of roast beef, stacks of new potatoes piled like shot at Woolwich, and the actual Haycock, quite at home in caring for a large part of the parish, and specially delighting in parcelling out clumps of pudding to boys who frolicked and gambolled round the tables'. (Lynn Advertiser, 24th February 1872).
60. NRO. SF231
61. In 1835 the soon to be Queen Victoria passed though the town on her way to Holkham. She was greeted with such enthusiasm in London Road that she was forced to take refuge for a time in a house in Buckingham Terrace, but which one is not recorded.
62. Ekwall, p239
63. NRO. C/Sca2/131
64. NRO. DN/TA137
65. Armes refers to Haycock as, 'one of the antique celebrities of old Lynn, a right good man with a considerable income, who made no haste to be rich; was kind to his servants; extremely hospitable; wore the breeches and buckles of the period, and appeared in his place duly every morning to join a party to hot sausages at 11 at the Rose and Crown, and again at the same place at eight in the evening, where with long pipes and "glasses round" the same party, swelled by other southern citizens, became enveloped in a dense cloud of smoke, so dense as to be impenetrable to the eye of an intruder; and indeed often, what with smoke and what with brandy, the individuals seated round the table could scarcely see each other'. (Lynn Advertiser, 24th February 1872).
66. Armes. Lynn Advertiser, 24th February 1872
67. King's Lynn Poor Law Union, C/GP/13/322-336
68. Armes. Lynn Advertiser, 24th February 1872
69. Thew, p15
70. NRO. DN/TA861
71. NRO. BL IXb/19
72. King's Lynn Poor Law Union, C/GP/13/377-391
73. NRO.DN/TA861
74. Lynn Advertiser, 8th January 1853
76. Deeds in possession of Mr. Bernie Ransom
77. These photographs were published by Bob Booth in 2006

Bibliography

Aikin, J.W. Reminiscences of Lynn, Advertising Herald, 1866.

Armes, William. Memories of Lynn, The Lynn Advertiser, 24th February 1872 and subsequent issues. (Reprinted by The Friends of King's Lynn Local History Library in 1990).

Barton, Colin. Yards and Courts of Lynn, West Norfolk Local History Society Journal Vol I, Part 3, 1979

Beloe, E.M. Our Borough: Our Churches, Macmillan and Bowes, 1899

Booth, Bob. King's Lynn in the 1930s, Tricky Sam Publishing, 2006

Burnet, W.P. A Hand-Book of King's Lynn, Whittaker and Co, 1846

Chadwick, John Nurse. Memorials of the Vicarage House & Garden in South Lynn, King's Lynn, 1851

Clarke, Helen and Carter, Alan. Excavations in King' Lynn 1963-1970, London, 1977

Coulton, J.J. Recollections of Lynn, The Lynn Advertiser, 20th November 1880

Defoe, Daniel. A Tour through the Whole Island of Great Britain, Penguin edition, 1971

Ekwall, Eilert. The Concise Oxford Dictionary of English Place Names, Oxford, 1936

Grisenthwaite, J. Remarks on the Political Economy and Management of the Poor in the Borough of King's Lynn. King's Lynn, 1811

Higgins, David. The Early Nineteenth Century Reshaping of King's Lynn. The Annual, No5, 1996. (Bulletin of the Norfolk Archaeological and Historical Research Group).

Higgins, David. The Antiquities of King's Lynn, Phoenix Publications, 2001

Higgins, David. The ingenious Mr. Henry Bell, Phoenix Publications, 2005

Hillen, Henry. History of the Borough of King's Lynn, Norwich, 1907

Lee, William. Report on a Preliminary Inquiry into… the Sanitary Condition… of the Inhabitants of the Borough of King's Lynn, 1852

Municipal Corporation Boundaries, King's Lynn Report, c1835 (ordered to be printed 1837)

Owen, Dorothy, (Ed). The Making of King's Lynn, London, 1984

Parker, Vanessa. The Making of King's Lynn, Phillimore, 1971

Richards, Paul. King's Lynn, Phillimore, 1990

Richards, William. The History of Lynn, King's Lynn, 1812

Thew, John Dyker. Personal Recollections, 1891. (Reprinted from the Lynn Advertiser),

Webb, Sidney and Beatrice. English Local Government: Statutory Authorities for Special Purposes, Longmans, 1922

Woodward, Sir Llewellyn. The Age of Reform 1815-1870, Oxford, 1938

INDEX

Aberdeen 13
Aberdeen Street 109
Abraham, John 49,67
Adams, Charles 84
Adcock, George 78
Aggar, William 90
Aikman, John 36
Aitkin, John 53
Albert (Prince) 102
Albert Street 51,60,102,103
Alberta (ship) 57
Albion Place 50
Albion Street 55,107,120
Alexandra Dock 112
All Saint's Church 120
All Saint's Street 27,51,66,68
Allen, Maxey 26
Allen, Stephen 7,22
Allen, Thomas 36,82
Almshouse Road 99
Andrews, Mary Ann 56
Angel Inn 37
Archaeological Survey 1,114
Armes, John 70
Armes, William 49,58,63,66,70,87,90,92,110,120-122
Arthur Street 74
Athenaeum 41,61
Athenaeum Chambers 42
Austin Street 39,40,51,102,114
Australia 58
Ayre, William 50,67,119

Bagge 7,31,55,104-106,121
Bagge, Edward 54,104
Bagge, Richard 37,55,59,60,104,106,107,120
Bagge, Thomas 30,33,35-37
Bagge, William 104
Bailey, William 78
Baker Lane 9,34,43,114
Ballast Boat PH 33
Bankruptcy Court 58
Barnett, Henry 55,105
Batterham, Mr 36
Baxter's Bridge 43
Baxter's Plain 41,120
Beast Market 8,42
Bedford Street 55,90
Begley Francis 120
Begley, Thomas 24,63
Begley's Row 82
Belgrave Hotel 57,106

Bell, Elizabeth 67
Bell, Henry (Architect) 34,37,112
Bell, Henry (Mayor) 6,67
Beloe, Edward Milligan 117
Benn, William 71
Bennett, Charles 45
Bentinck Dock 112
Bentinck Street 51,91,112
Bentinck, William 42
Birmingham 53
Bishop's Lynn 3
Black Boy Street 9,25
Black Horse Street 39,40
Blackburn, Mr 28
Blackburne, Thomas 119
Blackfriars Hall 42
Blackfriars Pasture 55,104,120
Blackfriars Friary 104
Blackfriars Road 54,55,106
Blackfriars Street 46,104,121
Blencoe 7
Boal Street 113
Board of Guardians 15,44,101,117
Board of Health 12
bone burning 60
Boothby, Mary Ann 71
Borough Treasurer 45
Boston 7,14
Bowling Green PH 88
Brick Kiln Road 108
brickmaking 60
brickyard 78
Brickyard, The 108
Bridge Street 27,113
Brin, Mary 23
Britton, Thomas 87
Broad Street 9,41,42,56,114
Broadway, Edward 84,89
Brown, Candler 99
Brown, James 38,64
Brunton, John 24
Buckingham Terrace 50,59,60,80,81,94,120-121
Buckingham, Thomas 80
Building regulations 12,14,108
Burcham, Mrs 70
Burn, Rev 22
Burnet, William 53
Burtons 17
Bush, Thomas 25

Cade, Mary 78
Cade's Garden 50,78,114
Campbell's Soup 113
Camperdown 119

Candler, William 44,51,59,74,91
Carter, Ann 18
Cary, Alderman 41
Carus-Wilson, Prof Eleanor 117
Castle Hill, Caithness 13
Castle Rising 120
Cattle Market 42,54
Chadwick, John Nurse 55,68,121
Chadwick Street 55,68
Chamberlain, Town 4,6,8,24,39,118
Chapel Street 39,40,56,102,114
Chase, The 99,100
Chase Road 110
Checker, John 120
Checker, Richard 51,71,88,120,121
Checker Street 33,51,70,81,87,88,120,121
Chequer, Little 33
Chequer Street 9,29,34,36
Chesterton, Dame Elizabeth 114
Chesterton, Report 114
cholera 11
Church Commissioners 31
Church Street 9,28,114
Civic Amenities Act 1967 114
Clenchwarton 120
Clifton House 33,46
Clough Bridge 44
Clough Fleet 43
Clough Fleet Tunnel 45
Clough Garden 51,91,92,99,114
Coburg Street 110,111
Coffee Tavern 119
Colby's Yard 64
Colchester 119
Cole Street 111
Common Staithe Quay 13
Coney, Walter 19
Conservation Area 114
Cook, Henry 68
Cook, Robert 68
Cooper, Joseph 101
Cooper Roller Bearings 112
Cooper, Thomas 17
Corn Exchange 37,61
Coronation (George IV) 49
Coronation Square 49-51,66-68,120
Corporation 3,4,6,12,16,21,23,24,26,27,33-35,37-45,
    50,54,57,59,78,82,99,100,110,112,113
Coulton, John James 12,55,117,119
Court Leet 4
Coward, John 19
Cox, Joseph 20
Coxedge, J 118
Crane, Thomas 30

Crawford, Jack 119
Cresswell, Mr 110
Cross Lane 25
Cross Street 91
Crown Inn, (Church Street) 9
Crown Inn, (London Road) 26,82
Crown Yard 48
Cruso and Maberley 61,110
Custom House 10
Cut Bridge 49

Dalsley's Yard 63
Dampgate Street 40
Dawes, Charles 25,36
Dawber, Matthew 32,119
Day, Thomas 32
Dean and Chapter (Norwich Cathedral) 30
Decay of Towns, (Statute of) 4
Defoe, Daniel 5
Demerara (ship) 57
Devil's Alley 30
Dilke Street 111
Dixon, Robert 49,63
Dixon, Robert (artist) 118
Dixon's Garden 63,114
Dobson, Isaac 89
Docks Railway 39
Dodman, Alfred 112
Dog Street 9,38
Doncaster, Matthew 64
Donthorne, William 37
Double Row 84
Douro Street 74
Dow Chemicals 113
Downham Market 71
Dyson, Thomas 100

Eagle Hotel 113
East Anglian Hotel 105
East Anglian Railway Company 55,110
East of England Banking Company 57
East Gate 9,40,84
East Street 102,112
Eau Brink Commissioners 54
Eau Brink Cut 48,49
Echo Road 54,89,104
Edmonton 56
Edward Street 83
Edwards, Rev Edward 7,22,24,36
Egypt (ship) 57
Eldred, Murray 20
Eldred's Corner 20
Elsden 7
Elsden, Edmund Rolfe 6,22

encroachment 5,8,13,17,18
Esk Terrace 82
Estray Pasture 38,42
Estuary Works 56
Ethel Terrace 113
Everard, Edward 40,51,58,59,94
Everard, Scarlet 31
Everard Street, North 51,57,60,94,95
Everard Street, South 51,94,95,109
Everard's Field 47,87,94
Exhibition Terrace 85
Exton's Road 56,57,101,108,109

Faden, William 4,9,16
Fanlights 61
Ffolkes family 50,58,66
Ffolkes' Garden 66,114
Ffolkes, Sir Martin Browne 67,84
Ffolkes, Sir William Browne 67
First New Town 38
First World War 112
Fisher Bridge 39
Fisher End 39
Fisher Fleet 3,39,43
Fison, Cornell 90
Foster, William Sharpe 28
Framingham's Almshouses 42,56
Frederick Place 64
Friars, The 25
Friar Street 27,51,87,88,113
Front Row 56,84
Fysh, James 35
Fyson, Joseph 67

Gant, Mr 27
Garden Row 51,70,71,84
Garner, Benjamin 71
Gas Manufactory 38
Gathergood, James 50,80,81
Gathergood, Maria 80,120
Gault brick 14
Gaywood 2,50,84,85,100,101,104,119
Gaywood Enclosure 84
Gaywood Hall 120
Gaywood Road 84
Gaywood Tithe Map 84
George IV 67
Gilbert Row 70
Gilbert, William 70
Goodwin Charles 50,51,54,60,82,91,99-102,118-120
Goodwin, Francis 22,24,118
Goodwin, Harvey 99,118,120
Goodwin's Fields 51,60,99,101
Goodwin's Road 47,51,61,99,120

Goulden, Susan 70
Graham Street 109
Grammar School House 82
Grand Festival 118
Grand Jury 6
Grass Market 17,40
Great Exhibition 85,111
Great Fire of London 14
Greyfriars 9,10,23,24
Gromitt, Thomas 64
Groom, Farndon 7,13
Grummett's Yard 64
Guanock Field 51,59,82,83,99
Guanock Gate 25,99,109
Guanock Place 49,50,61,82
Guanock Road 101
Guanock Row 50
Guanock Sea Bank 3,26
Guanock Terrace 50,70,71,82,99,100
Guardians of the Poor 57

Halifax, Thomas 67
Hall, John 64
Hall, Richard 68
Hamilton, Mrs 23
Hankinson, Rev 22
Hankinson, Robert 7
Hardwick Narrows 42
Hardwick Pits 26
Hardwick Road 100,101,113
Harrison, Roger 119
Harrod's Yard 63
Harwood, William 63
Hawkins, George 27,28
Haycock, Giles 80,81,87,88,121
Haycock's Garden 87
Henry VIII 2
Herbert de Losinga 2
High Bridge 17,18,20,42,43,45,46
High Street 13,17-21,40,46,48,117,119-120
Highgate 50,55,84,85,89,114
Hillington Hall 50,66
Hillington Row 50
Hillington Square 50,66-68
Hillyard, Francis 18
Hob in The Well PH 40
Hogg (e) 7,29
Holman, Charles Henry 110
Hopmans Way (Lane) 39,40
hopper heads 15
Hospital Walk 50
Hye, Samuel 48

Improvement Commissioners 5

Jackson, Thomas 31
Jarvis, Sir Lewis Weston 51,59,88,121
Jarvis, Sir Lewis Whincop 32,33
Jary, Jacob 32
jettied buildings 4
Jewish Cemetery 49,66
Jews Lane 48
John, (King) 3
John Street 95
Johnson, William 35,107
Johnson's Court 102
Judd, John 20

Keed, John 55,91
Keppel, Major George 74
Keppel Street 51,74
kimmeridge clay 14
King Street 9,15,29,34,36,48,88,117,120
King, Thomas 64
King's Lynn 1,3-8,12,14,47,53,56,58,84,99,
   101,104,112,114,119
King's Staithe Lane 33,35
King's Staithe Square 35
Kirby Street 51,89,90,118
Kirby's Ground 55,89,90,114

Ladybridge 27-29,32
Ladybridge Chapel 28
Ladybridge House 31
Laird, John 36,68
Laird, William 36
lamp pillar 38
lane 7
latching 4
Lath Street 9,29,33
Lavenham 4
Laurence, William 55,90
Leadenhall Lane 32
Lee, John 35
Lee, William 12,44,57
Lenn, The 3
lime burning 60
listed buildings 61
Little Downham 120
Littleport Bridge 40
Littleport Street 40
London 5,24,84,83
London Overspill Agreement 1,113
London Road (The New Road) 8,10,15,16,21,25,27,35,
   40,42,47, 49-51,54,58,60,61,63,64,67,68,70,71,74,
   80, 81,87,88,94,95,104,113,118,120-121
London Road Brewery 71
Long Walk 101
Lower Canada 56,59-61,110,111,114

Lynn Conversazione and Arts Society 42,63
Lynn and Dereham Railway 53,54,120
Lynn ditches 94
Lynn and Ely Railway 53,54,104,120
Lynn Museum 45,107
Lynn Station 54

Maberley, William 37,41
Macedonia (ship) 57
Malam, John 38
Manchester Town Hall 118
Market Cross 37
Market House 37,118
Market Street 55,107
Marsh Cut 39,47,54,56
Marshall Street 51,55,90
Marshall, Thomas 50,51,74,89,90,102,119
Marshall's Garden 55,74,114
Marshall's Orchard 99,102,114
Mary, Queen 3
Mayor and Burgesses 19
Medlock, George 94
Melbourne Street 51,91
Melvin, Robert 36
Middleton, Barnard 84
Middleton, Elizabeth 84
Middleton, John 70,71
Middleton Meadow 70,114
Middleton Stop Drain 82
Miles, William 110
Mill Lane 27
Miller's Entry 30
Millfleet 3,7,26-28,38,43,49,50,67,112
Millfleet Terrace 50,67
Mitchley, Edward 70
Monkwearmouth 120
Mott, Robert 56,61,107,110,111
Municipal Corporation Act 1835 11
Murrell, John 78

naming (street) 12,15
Napoleonic Wars 15,49
Navvies 47,56
Nelson Street 9,15, 29-31,114
New Conduit Street 12,18,41-43,45,46,114
New Road (see London Road)
New Walk 25
Newham, Samuel 8,19,37,118
Newham, William 8,18,22,24,48,50,61,63,70,74,
   80,89,102,118-120
Newland 3
Newton, Rev Robert 25
Norfolk 8
Norfolk Estuary Company 39,54

norfolk reds 14
Norfolk Street 13,15,17-20,40,47,48,51,54,89,90,102,
    104,113,120
North Clough Lane 43,45,46,59,104
North End 38,39,41,118
North Sea 112
North Street 9,38,78,95,114
Norwich, Bishop of 3
Norwich, Cathedral Priory 3
Norwich, Theatre Circuit 24
Numbering houses 12,15

Ockley, Simon 107,108
'Old Porsley' 119
Old Town 1
Ouse Lane 32,33
Oxley William 31

Page, Samuel 108
Page Stair Lane 35
Palmer, John 50,78
Paradise Lane 41,42,102
Paradise Pasture 42
Parlett, William 18,19
Parliament 6,8,9
Partridge, Frederick 54,91,120
Pashley Street 74
Paving Acts 1,6,9,14,29,59,60,108
    1803 (First Act) 7-9,14,15,25,26,37,39,42
    1806 (Second Act) 8,9,14,30,38,48
    1859 12
Paving Commissioners (Lynn) 1,7-9,12-16,18-41,
    43-46,49,57-59,64,67,74,78,80,88-90,94,95,102,103,
    105,108,109,111,112,114
Paving Committee 7
Paviors 12,13
Paxton Terrace 111
Peel Street 109
Pentney, Peter 45
Peto and Betts 54
Pierrepoint Drain 110
Pilot Street 38,48,114,118
plat band 60
Pleasant Row 74
Plough PH 37
poor rate books 91
Popjoy, William 13
Portland Street 47,55,59-61,104,105
Portland Street, North 105
Portland Street, South 105
Primitive Methodist Chapel 67,85
Providence Street 48,49,63,64,67
public health 11
Public Health Act 1872 12

Public Health Inquiry 57
public privy 32
Purdy, James 41,60,90,107
Purdy, William 41,60,90
Purfleet 3,10,12,34,38,41-45,49,54,104,119
Purfleet Bridge 32-35
Purfleet Place 33-35
Purfleet Street 9,36,43,46,114,119
Pursglove, Robert 32,39,119

Quakers 58,59,60,80, 81,121
Quaker's Ground 50,80
Quarter Sessions 6,18-20,28
Queen Street 15,29,33-35,48,117

railway mania 53
Railway Road 47,55,58-61,90,104,105,107
Railway Station 54,55
Railway Street 55,105
Red Cow Street 28
Regent Street 51,91
Reid Street 111
Reynolds, Francis Kirby 120
Richards, William 15,28,48
Richardson, William 51,71
Richardson, Sarah 71
Rolfe, John Jex 71
Rolin, Ann 56
Rolin Daniel 56
Rolin, Thomas Bateley 57
Rolin William Salmon 55-58,60,78,95,106,108,109,
    113,120
Rose and Crown PH 121
rounded corner 31,39
Royal Oak PH 36
Russell, Bedford 90
Russell Place 91
Russell Street 51,109

St. Ann's Street 38
St. George's Guildhall 24
St. James' Chapel 3,4
St. James' School 67
St. James' Street 7,8,13,23-25,28,82
St. James' Workhouse 25,107
St. James' Road 91,104
St. John's Church 43,44,120
St. John's Street 51,95
St. John's Terrace 43,47,55,57,59,61,106,107,109,113
St. Margaret's Church 3,7,9,21,118,119
St. Margaret's Parish 6,15
St. Margaret's Place 29,32,33
St. Nicholas Chapel 3,56
St Nicholas Street 38,39,114

Saers Marsh 99
Saturday Market 8,21
Saturday Market Place 13,17,18,21,23,118
Savage, Frederick 112
Sayer, George Frederick 33
Seapey, William 74
Second New Town 34
Sedgeford Lane 25,42,43,45,114
Self 7,29
Sexton's House 21, 22,118
Shakespeare PH 36
Shambles 37
Sheppard, John 20,118
Sheringham 112
Shoulder of Mutton Piece 70
Siege of Lynn 108
Simpson, William Smith 54,55,105,120
Slum Clearance 47
Slum Clearance Committee 113
Smetham, John 64
Smith, Alexander 34
 Smith, William 18,49,63
Society of Mediaeval Archaeology 117
South Clough Lane 43,59,91,92
South Gate 7-9,25,26,28,38,42,48,57,82
South Lynn 3,18,27,47,49,51,67,68,78,80,87,94,
   119,120
South Lynn Tithe Map 100,108
South Street 50,78,94,95,113
South Wootton 26
Southgate Street 27,80,120
Southwell, John 51,71,91
Spinner (Lane) Row 41
Spurn Head 13
Stag Row 85
stallage 21
Stanley Street 55,60,90
Station Road 105
Station Street 105
Stepney Baptist Chapel 104
Stonegate Street 27
street lighting 38
Sugar's Almshouses 120
Sugars, John 57,61,63,64,67,94,120
Superintendent Registrar 12,56
Surrey Street 114
Swaffham 37,81

Taylor's Yard 64
Temperance Hall 104
Tennyson Avenue 99
Terrace Walk 82,108
Theatre Royal 24,118
Thew, John Dyker 99,101

Thomas Street 83
Three Cranes PH 31
Three Crowns Street 29,33
Three Pigeon Street 23
Todd, George 31
Tower Gardens 23
Tower Place 23,24
Tower Street 9,23,25,41,43,48,91
Town Development Act 1952 113
Town Dues Office 35
Town Expansion 1,47,56
Town Hall 21
Town Improvement 1,11,34
Town Improvement Clauses Act 1847 12
Triance, William 51,74
Trinity Chapel 9,21,22,118
Trundle, Edmund 50,59,81
Tuck, James 20
Tuck, William 6
Tuesday Market Place 17,18,37,42,49,114,118,120,120
Turbe, Bishop 2
Turner 109
Turner, William 34
Turnpike Trustees 117

Union Baptist Chapel 107
Union Lane 21
Union Place 89,90
Union Street 51,66,68
Urban Sanitary Authority 33

Valiant Sailor PH 30,31,119
Valinger's Place 64
Valinger's Road 49,51,61,63,64,94,95,113
Vancouver Avenue 101
Vancouver Centre 1
Vicarage (St. Margaret's) 32,33
Vicarage (South Lynn) 68,121
Vicarage Lane 50,68
Victoria, (Queen) 102,121
Victoria Street 51,74

Wales, Joseph 66,68
Walks, The 43,82,99
Walker, Edward 78,107
Wallington Hall 67
Walters, John 118
Walton, William 25
Wanford, Robert 64
Wash (The) 39
Watering, James 71
Waterloo Street 55,106
Waterspouts 31
Watson, Richard 23

Wellesley Street 55,105,106
Wellington, Duke of 15,74,106
Wellington Street 55,74
Welsh slate 14,63
Wenn's 18,21,49
Wesleyan Chapel 25
West Street 74
West Winch 120
Westminster 5
Whin family 91
Whincop, George Raynor 91
Whincop Place 55,92
Whincop, Robert 6-8,91
Whincop Street 55,92
Whitby Thomas 71,78
White Hart Inn 28
Whitmore, Mr 118
Wiggenhall 119
Williams, John 54,120
William Street 82
Wilson, Francis Reed 120
Winder, Rev William 9
Windsor Road 49,51,55,70,71,74,100
Windsor Place 74,101
Windsor Row 51,71
Wisbech 120
Wood Street 50,78,113,121
Woods 26
Woods, Thomas 78
World War II 78,113
Wrestler's Street 35
Wright, Charles 63
Wright, James 67,110
Wyatt, James 118
Wyatt Street 111

Yards (The) 47,48,119
Yarmouth, Great 112
Young England (ship) 57

Zeppelins 112